SCOTS-IRISH LINKS

1575–1725

PART FIVE

07-1897

by
David Dobson

CLEARFIELD

Printed for
Clearfield Company by
Genealogical Publishing Co.
Baltimore, Maryland
2006

Reprinted for
Clearfield Company by
Genealogical Publishing Co.
Baltimore, Maryland
2007

ISBN-13: 978-0-8063-5301-2
ISBN-10: 0-8063-5301-5

Made in the United States of America

INTRODUCTION

The Plantation of Ulster by Scots in the seventeenth century is a well-established fact. Genealogists, however, require very specific reference material which is generally missing from the published accounts of the migration of up to 100,000 Scottish Lowlanders to northern Ireland at that time.

Part Five of *Scots-Irish Links, 1575-1725* attempts to identify some of these Scots settlers and is based mainly on contemporary primary source material found in Ireland and in Scotland. A feature of this volume is the inclusion of a number of shipmasters from Ulster trading with west of Scotland ports. It is highly likely that they were residents of the port to which the ship belonged and that the skipper owned part of the vessel. The book also identifies more young men from Ulster who were either serving apprenticeships in Scotland or studying at university. These men on their return to Ireland would become in due course the elite of the Ulster-Scots communities there.

Within a few generations, the descendants of these Ulster Scots emigrated in substantial numbers across the Atlantic where, as the Scotch-Irish, they made a major contribution to the settlement and development of Colonial America.

David Dobson
St Andrews, Scotland

SCOTS-IRISH LINKS

REFERENCES

Archives

AA	=	Ayr Archives
ACA	=	Aberdeen City Archives
BL	=	British Library, London
ECA	=	Edinburgh City Archives
HMC	=	Historical Manuscript Commission
NAS	=	National Archives of Scotland
PRONI	=	Public Record Office, Northern Ireland

Publications

AGA	=	Acts of the General Assembly of the Church of Scotland, 1648-1842, [Edinburgh, 1843]
APS	=	Acts of the Parliament of Scotland, [Edinburgh, 1870]
CLC	=	The Lag Charters, [Edinburgh, 1958]
CPR	=	Calendar of Patent and Close Rolls of Chancery in Ireland, [Dublin, 1863]
CSPIre	=	Calendar of State Papers, Ireland
CTP	=	Calendar of Treasury Papers
DAL	=	Dalton's English Army Lists, [London, 1960]
DBR	=	Dumfries Burgh Records
GA	=	Records of the General Assemblies of the Church of Scotland, 1648-1649.[Edinburgh, 1896]
GBR	=	Glasgow Burgess Roll
HMC	=	Historical Manuscript Commission
HS	=	History of Scots, [Edinburgh, 1999]
ISC	=	Ireland In the Seventeenth Century, [London, 1884]
MA	=	The MacDonnells of Antrim, [Belfast, 1874]
MRBI	=	Muniments of the Royal Burgh of Irvine, [Edinburgh, 1891]
MUG	=	Munimenta Universitatis Glasguensis, 1450-1727, Volume III, [Glasgow, 1854]
PES	=	An Account of the Proceedings of the Estates in Scotland, 1689-1690, [Edinburgh, 1955]
REA	=	Register of Apprentices of the City of Edinburgh, 1583-1666, 1666-1700, [Edinburgh, 1906/1929]
RGSU	=	Records of the General Synod of Ulster, 1691-1820, [Belfast, 1890]
RPCS	=	Register of the Privy Council of Scotland, series

SLT   =   Records of the Synod of Lothian and Tweeddale,
               1640-1641, [Edinburgh, 1977]

WDSD =   Walker's Diary of the Siege of Derry, 1688-1689,
               [Londonderry, 1895] pp68-74

The Ulster branch of the family of Wauchope, G.M.Wauchope,
    London, 1929

SCOTS-IRISH LINKS,

1575-1725.

[Part Five]

ABERCROMBIE, or CROMWELL, ADAM, born 1560, of Killelerty, County Down, 1633. [CSPIre#CCLXX/45]

ABERCROMBIE, ALEXANDER, Cornet of the Royal Regiment of Dragoons of Ireland in 1696. [DAL.IV.119]

ABERCROMBIE, JAMES, in Limerick, 7 February 1700. [NAS.GD406.1.4735]

ABERCROMBIE, ROBERT, a quartermaster with 35 years military experience, late in the Queen of Bohemia's service, petitioned for command of the fort at Culmore, near Londonderry, in 1635. [CSPIre#CCLXXVI/80]

ABERCROMBY, THOMAS, in County Leitrim, 1631. [CPR#586]

ACHESON, Sir ARCHIBALD, of Clancairney, was admitted as a baronet of Nova Scotia on 1 January 1628. [NAS.BNS#73]

ACHESON, Sir GEORGE, 1629-1685. [PRONI#LPC.1372]

ACHESON, JAMES, planned for the erection of a Mint in Ireland 1625. [CSPIre#CCLXVIII]

ACHESON, LUKE, in Tullyhogue, County Tyrone, 1610. [Tullyhogue Muster Roll]

ACHESON, PATRICK, in Omagh, 1666. [Hearth Money Roll]

ACHMOOTY, ARTHUR, Quartermaster of the Horse in the North of Ireland 22 March 1675, quartered in Mollingar in August 1677. [HMC.Ormonde#II, 203, 207]

ADAIR, ARCHIBALD, formerly Dean of Raphoe, County Donegal, appointed Bishop of Killally and Achonry, in the province of Connaught, 1629. [CPR#522/537]

ADAIR, Sir ROBERT, 1659-1745. [PRONI#T732/24]

ADAIR, Sir ROBERT, of Kinhilt, petitioned the Scots Parliament for losses incurred by him in Ireland, 1640. [APS.V.324]; petitioned the General Assembly of the Church of Scotland on 5 August 1643. [AGA#74]

ADAIR, ROBERT, to swear in parish constables for the parish of St Connor in Ireland, 5 July 1631. [NAS.GD97.Sec.1/409]

ADAIR, Sir WALTER, of Ballymenoch, son and heir apparent of Anna Helena Scott or Edmonstone, 23 October 1696. [NAS.GD97.576]

ADAIR, WILLIAM, master of the Prosperity of Belfast at Port Glasgow in October 1689. [NAS.E72.19.15]

ADAM, JOHN, master of the Mayflower of Belfast, arrived in Glasgow on 24 June 1684 from Belfast. [NAS.E72.19.9]

ADARE, THOMAS, surgeon of the Londonderry Regiment of Foot in 1689. [DAL.III.83]

AGNEW, ALEXANDER, son of Alexander Agnew in Ireland, was apprenticed to Robert Selkirk, a merchant in Edinburgh, on 27 August 1679. [REA]

AGNEW, JOHN, master and merchant of the Anna of Portaferry arrived in the Clyde from Belfast in October 1695. [NAS.E72.19.23]

AGNEW, Sir PATRICK, 1661. [PRONI#D265/3]

AGNEW, PATRICK, 1700-1725. [PRONI#D282/4]

AGNEW, ROBERT, master of the Andrew of Belfast arrived in Port Glasgow on 31 January 1682 from Spain; from Port Glasgow to Belfast on 31 January 1682; at Port Patrick in December 1682; master of the Andrew of Belfast, arrived in Glasgow on 10 May 1689 from Belfast. [NAS.E72.19.5/6/14; E72.20.8]

AICKIN, ALEXANDER, born in County Down, brown hair, trooper of the King's Guard of Horse from 1676. [HMC.Ormonde.II.237]

ALEXANDER, JAMES, a minister in Ireland, 1689. [NAS.CH2.1284.2/44-52]

ALEXANDER, JOHN, son of John Alexander in County Monaghan, was apprenticed to David Cathcart of Glendaish, a merchant in Edinburgh, on 28 June 1699. [REA]

ALEXANDER, JOHN, a Scots-Irish student at Glasgow University in 1701. [MUG#172]

ALEXANDER, Sir WILLIAM, in Dacostroose and Portlagh, County Donegal, 1627; of Menstrie, Scotland, purchased lands in County Donegal from Sir James Cunningham of Glengarnock, Scotland, on 26 February 1628; he was also granted Mullalelish, in the barony of O'Neilan, County Armagh, on 14 January 1628. [CPR#267/384/439]

ALGEO, ROBERT, possibly from Renfrewshire, by 1614 the factor in Strabane for Sir Claud Hamilton of Schawfield. [Artigarvan stone] [PRONI.T544; NLI.ms8014/ix; BL.Add. MS4770/94]

ALLAN, FRANCIS, the collector at Donaghadie, was admitted as a burgess and guilds-brother of Ayr on 19 February 1696. [Ayr Burgess Roll]

ALLAN, JOHN, leased lands of Ballibrie and Ballimainstra, Grayabbeylands, from William Edmonstone of Braichland on 16 October 1623. [NAS.GD97.Sec.1/378]

ALLAN, JOHN, master of the Anna of Larne arrived at Larne on 5 January 1669 from Larne. [NAS.E72.12.1]

ALLAN, PATRICK, with **Janet Vetch,** and their son **James Allan,** from Ireland to Dumfries by 1696. [NAS.CH2.537.15.1/161-165]

ALLAN, ROBERT, master of the Elizabeth of Londonderry at Port Glasgow in December 1690, also in March 1691. [NAS.E72.19.21]

ALLEN, J., an Irish student at Glasgow University in 1705. [MUG#182]

ALLIOT, RICHARD, a Scots-Irish student at Glasgow University in 1703. [MUG#177]

ANDERSON, ANDREW, a printer in Edinburgh was granted the monopoly of printing bibles and psalm books for the Church of Ireland for 41 years, in 1672.[Acts of the Parliament of Scotland, Volume VIII, fo.206]

ANDERSON, DAVID, killed by rebels at Tully Castle, County Fermanagh, on 25 December 1641. See Patrick Hume's deposition. [ISC.I.215]

ANDERSON, JAMES, killed by rebels at Tully Castle, County Fermanagh, on 25 December 1641. See Patrick Hume's deposition. [ISC.I.215]

ANDERSON, JANET, a widow, returned to Dumfries from Ireland in 1691. [NAS.CH2.537.15.1/73-94]

ANDERSON, JOHN, merchant and passenger on the Blessing of Dunalady arrived in Ayr on 20 March 1673 from Dublin. [NAS.E72.3.3]

ANDERSON, JOHN, minister at Glenarme, 1684. [NAS.NRAS#231/12/355]

ANDERSON, JOHN, a Captain of the Londonderry Regiment of Foot in 1689. [DAL.III.83]

ANDERSON, JOHN, from Ireland, in Penningham in 1710. [Penningham KSR:23.8.1710]

ANDERSON, THOMAS, killed by rebels at Tully Castle, County Fermanagh, on 25 December 1641. See Patrick Hume's deposition. [ISC.I.215]

ANDERSON, WILLIAM, a skipper from Limekilns, imprisoned in Ireland, 1647. [APS,VI.i.718]

ANDERSON, WILLIAM, quarter-master of a Londonderry or Inniskilling Regiment in 1690. [DAL.III.168]

ARBUCKLE, JAMES, a merchant in Belfast, was admitted as a burgess and guilds-brother of Glasgow on 6 June 1715. [GBR]

ARBUCKLE, WILLIAM, merchant on the Marigold of Belfast from Port Glasgow to Madeira in December 1690. [NAS.E72.19.22]

ARBUCKLE, WILLIAM, son of James Arbuckle a merchant in Belfast, was admitted as a burgess and guilds-brother of Glasgow on 6 June 1715. [GBR]

ARCHIBALDSON, ROBERT STEWART, a merchant in Ballintoy, Ireland, 1671. [Rothesay Town Council Records, 23.10.1671]

ARDOCH, ADAM, a defender at the Siege of Derry, 29 July 1689. [WDSD]

ARMOR, EDWARD, a Scots-Irish student at Glasgow University in 1702. [MUG#175]

ARMSTRONG, JOHN, was murdered near Lissan by rebels in 1641. [ISC.I.287]

ARMSTRONG, JOHN, sr., soldier of Colonel Bayly's Company in February 1648. [HMC.Ormonde.II.70]

ARMSTRONG, JOHN, jr., soldier of Colonel Bayly's Company in February 1648. [HMC.Ormonde.II.69]

ARMSTRONG, Sir THOMAS, 1624-1684. [PRONI#T580/55]

ARMSTRONG, THOMAS, a Captain of the Inniskilling Regiment of Foot at Dundalk in October 1689. [DAL.III.122]

ARMSTRONG, ..., possibly a Captain of the Inniskilling Regiment of Horse in 1689, killed near Cavan on 12 February 1690. [DAL.III.27/28/122]

ARNOTT, GEORGE, Captain of the Earl of Dunbarton's Regiment at Kinsale in April 1679. [HMC.Ormonde.II.219]

ARTHUR, CHARLES, master and merchant of the Charles of Belfast arrived in Port Glasgow on 2 September 1691 from Montserrat. [NAS.E72.19.21]

ARTHUR, ROBERT, master and merchant of the Jane and Sarah of Belfast from the Clyde to Belfast on 3 March 1691. [NAS.E72.19.22]

ASHMORE, SAMUEL, an Anglo-Irish student at Glasgow University in 1702. [MUG#174]

AUCHINLEK, ROBERT, chaplain to the Inniskilling Dragoons in 1689. [DAL.III.35]

AUCHMUTY, JOHN, was commissioned as a Captain of the Inniskilling Regiment of Horse on 20 July 1689, later of Newtown-Flood, County Longford, died in 1722. [DAL.III.27/28]

AUCHMUTY, ..., surgeon of the Inniskilling Regiment of Horse, 1696. [DAL.IV.117]

BABBINGTON, RICHARD, an Anglo-Irish student at Glasgow University in 1700. [MUG#169]

BAILLIE, DAVID, Lieutenant of the Earl of Dunbarton's Regiment at Kinsale in April 1679. [HMC.Ormonde.II.219]

BAILLIE, THOMAS, a burgess of Killileagh, 17 November 1612. [CSPIre#Carte pp62/110]

BAILLIE, WILLIAM, a burgess of Strabane, County Tyrone, 25 November 1612. [CSPIre#Carte.pp62/117]

BAILLIE, WILLIAM, granted a patent of denization also lands in County Cavan – the manor of Baillieborough - on 22 June 1629. [CPR#476]

BAILLY. ANDREW, a defender at the Siege of Derry, 29 July 1689. [WDSD]

BAILLY, JOHN, a defender at the Siege of Derry, 29 July 1689. [WDSD]; an Ensign of the Londonderry Regiment of Foot in 1689. [DAL.III.83]

BAIRD, JOHN, soldier of Colonel Bayly's Company in February 1648. [HMC.Ormonde.II.70]

BAIRD, JOHN, Ensign of the Inniskilling Regiment of Foot in 1693. [DAL.III.336]

BAIRD, ROBERT, a Lieutenant of the Inniskilling Regiment of Foot, 1696. [DAL.IV.145]

BALFOUR, DAVID, born in Scotland before 1603, settled in County Tyrone. [CPR#99]

BALFOUR, Lord JAMES, granted lands in County Fermanagh – the manor of Carrowshee – also to him and his wife Anne were granted lands in County Fermanagh – the manor of Legan – on 6 October 1629. [CPR#479][CSPIre#CCLXXVII/36]

BALFOUR, WILLIAM, 1619-1640. [PRONI#T581{Vol.iv, 157}]

BANKHEAD, JAMES, a Scots-Irish student at Glasgow University in 1700. [MUG#169]

BANNERMAN, GEORGE, Lieutenant of the Earl of Dunbarton's Regiment at Kinsale in April 1679. [HMC.Ormonde.II.219]

BANNERMAN, JAMES, minister of Baltimore, Ireland, fled to Scotland by 1642. [SLT#150]

BARCLAY, ANDREW, Ensign of the Earl of Dunbarton's Regiment at Kinsale in April 1679. [HMC.Ormonde.II.219]

BARCLAY, GAVIN, the Precentor of Cashel was appointed a vicar in the Diocese of Cashel on 20 May 1629. [CPR#444]

BARCLAY, HUGH, rector of Dromore, 1631. [CPR#593]

BARCLAY, JAMES, master of the Margaret of Donaghadie at Port Patrick on 28 July 1682. [NAS.E72.20.7]

BARCLAY, ROBERT, 1648-1690. [PRONI#T100062/45/70]

BARCLAY, WILLIAM, a burgess of Newton Ards, County Down, 17 January 1612. [CSPIre.Carte pp62/84]

BARCLAY, WILLIAM, Lieutenant of the Earl of Dunbarton's Regiment at Kinsale in April 1679. [HMC.Ormonde.II.219]

BARCLAY, WILLIAM, master of the William of Hollywood from Port Glasgow on 6 January 1681 to Belfast; from Port Glasgow on 12 April 1681 bound for Belfast; arrived in Port Glasgow on 9 August 1681 from Belfast, from Port Glasgow to Belfast on 14 October 1681; arrived from Belfast on 29 November 1681; from Port Glasgow to Belfast on 25 December 1681; arrived in Port Glasgow on 15 February 1682 from Belfast; arrived in Port Glasgow on 15 August 1682 from Belfast; from Port Glasgow to Belfast on 30 August 1682; arrived in Port Glasgow on 20 October 1682 from Belfast; from Port Glasgow to Belfast on 14 March 1682; from Port Glasgow to Belfast on 9 November 1682; from Port Glasgow to Belfast on 6 April 1683; arrived in Port Glasgow on 26 July 1683 from Dublin. [NAS.E72.19.2/3/4/5/6/8]

BARNET, ALEXANDER, an Irish student at Glasgow University in 1704. [MUG#180]

BARR, ROBERT, keeper of Culmore Castle on the River Foyle, and his son Gabriel, pre 1649 but undated. [CSPIre#cclxxvi/125]

BARRY, JAMES, killed by rebels at Tully Castle, County Fermanagh, on 25 December 1641. See Patrick Hume's deposition. [ISC.I.215]

BATTY, HENRY, an Anglo-Irish student at Glasgow University in 1701. [MUG#172]

BAXTER, JOHN, a Scots-Irish student at Glasgow University in 1703. [MUG#177]

BAYERS, JAMES, master and merchant of the Janet of Donachadie from Irvine to Ireland on 26 July 1681. [NAS.E72.12.3]

BAYTY, JAMES, Tullyhogue, County Tyrone, 1610. [Tullyhogue Muster Roll]

BEGG, HENRY, was murdered by rebels in County Sligo in 1641. [ISC.I.365]

BELL, ADAM, with a sword and pike, Tullyhogue, County Tyrone, 1610. [Tullyhogue Muster Roll]

BELL, ADAM, Lieutenant of the Earl of Dunbarton's Regiment at Kinsale in April 1679. [HMC.Ormonde.II.219]

BELL, ALEXANDER, killed by rebels at Tully Castle, County Fermanagh, on 25 December 1641. See Patrick Hume's deposition. [ISC.I.215]

BELL, EDWARD, see deposition dated 5 May 1653. [ISC.I.268]

BELL, HEW, master of the Jean of Belfast, arrived in Port Patrick on 28 August 1682; arrived in Port Glasgow on 2 January 1683 from Belfast; from Port Glasgow to Belfast on 29 January 1683. [NAS.E72.20.7; E72.19.8]

BELL, HUMPHREY, a Captain of the Londonderry Regiment of Foot in 1689. [DAL.III.83]

BELL, JENKIN, with a sword and pike, Tullyhogue, County Tyrone, 1610. [Tullyhogue Muster Roll]

BELL, JENKIN, in Tullyhogue, County Tyrone, 1610. [Tullyhogue Muster Roll]

BELL, THOMAS, a merchant in Dublin, 1690. [RPCS.XV.92]

BENNET, ..., a Protestant refugee from Londonderry 1689. [APES.I.77-79]

BERRY, ANDREW, in Tullyhogue, County Tyrone, 1610. [Tullyhogue Muster Roll]

BINGHAM, Captain **HENRY,** of Castlebar, County Mayo, was admitted as a baronet of Nova Scotia on 7 June 1634. [NAS.BNS#80]

BITLE, THOMAS, master of the Margaret of Donaghadie at Port Patrick on 2 August 1681. [NAS.E72.20.5]

BLACK, ROBERT, in Galway, 1615. [RPCS.XII.761]

BLACK, ROBERT, killed by rebels at Tully Castle, County Fermanagh, on 25 December 1641. See Patrick Hume's deposition. [ISC.I.215]

BLACK, VALENTINE, in Galway, 1615. [RPCS.XII.761]

BLACKBURN, WILLIAM, merchant of the Robert of Ballyshannon arrived in Port Glasgow in March 1691 from Killybegs; and of the Salmond of Coleraine arrived in the Clyde in February 1696 from Coleraine. [NAS.E72.19.21; E72.19.23]

BLACKSTOCK, WILLIAM, a merchant in Ireland, 1665. [DBR Burgh Court Processes]

BLAIN, or McBLAIN, DAVID, in Wester Knockbreck, Girvan, Ayrshire, formerly a merchant in Dublin, died in September 1717. [NAS.S/H]

BLAINE, ALEXANDER, a burgess of Strabane, County Tyrone, 25 November 1612. [CSPIre#Carte.pp62/117]

BLAIR, Cornet GEORGE, in Limerick, 1721.
[ECA.Moses.152/5937]

BLAIR, JAMES, a defender at the Siege of Derry, 29 July 1689.
[WDSD]

BLAIR, JAMES, a Scots-Irish student at Glasgow University in
1702. [MUG#174]

BLAIR, JOHN, yeoman in Coleraine, see deposition dated 8 March
1652. [ISC.I.245]

BLAIR, THOMAS, Lieutenant-Colonel of a Londonderry or
Inniskilling Regiment in 1690. [DAL.III.168]

BLAIR, THOMAS, merchant of the Merchant of Larne arrived in
the Clyde in December 1695 from Belfast. [NAS.E72.19.23]

BLAIR, WILLIAM, a Scots-Irish student at Glasgow University in
1703. [MUG#177]

BLIGH, ARCHIBALD, master of the Isabel of Dundee, arrived in
Kinsale on 26 February 1603 from Lisbon.
[CSPIre.CCXII/142]

BOLTON, THOMAS, master of the Nightingale of Belfast arrived
in Glasgow on 16 February 1686 from Dublin.
[NAS.E72.19.12]

BOYD, Colonel DAVID, died in Ulster by 1626. [CPR#156]

BOYD, FRANCIS, a defender at the Siege of Derry, 29 July 1689.
[WDSD]; a Lieutenant of the Londonderry Regiment of Foot
in 1689. [DAL.III.83]

BOYD, JOHN, merchant of the Mayflower of Donaghadie at Port
Patrick on 27 July 1682. [NAS.E72.20.7]

BOYD, JOHN, master of the Mayflower of Dublin, at Port Glasgow
in October 1689; master of the William of Belfast, a 100 ton
pink, from Belfast *with 30 passengers* to Virginia in 1699.
[NAS.E72.19.15][PRO.CO5.1441]

BOYD, JOHN, an Ensign of the Inniskilling Regiment of Foot, in 1691. [DAL.III.206]

BOYD, NATHANIEL, a Scots-Irish student at Glasgow University in 1705. [MUG#182]

BOYD, ROBERT, son and heir of Colonel David Boyd, to be made a free denizen of Ireland, 20 July 1626. [CPR#157]

BOYD, ROBERT, a resident of Glenarm in 1641, then a soldier under Captain Agnew, imprisoned in Carrickfergus, see deposition dated 4 May 1653. [ISC.I.275]

BOYD, ROBERT, master of the Margaret of Larne from Irvine to Ireland on 15 August 1681. [NAS.E72.12.5]

BOYD, ROBERT, a defender at the Siege of Derry, 29 July 1689. [WDSD]

BOYD, ROBERT, from Ireland to Dumfries in 1690. [NAS.CH2.537.15.1/34]

BOYD, THOMAS, leaseholder of Carncoggie, 24 February 1614, possibly husband of Eliza Smeton, died 15 August 1634, father of Hugh. [MA#440]

BOYD, THOMAS, a merchant in Belfast, 1691. [RPCS.XV.69]

BOYD, THOMAS, a Scots-Irish student at Glasgow University in 1702. [MUG#175]

BOYD, Captain WILLIAM, master of the Elizabeth of Coleraine, from Londonderry to Saltcoats, Ayrshire, and return in 1689. [RPCS

BOYD, Captain, was killed by the rebels at Lisnegarvy, 26 November 1641. [CSPIre#cclxxvii/67]

BRADY, WILLIAM, in Omagh, 1666. [Hearth Money Roll]

BRATTEN, THOMAS, a Scots-Irish student at Glasgow University in 1701. [MUG#172]

BREDIN, ISAAC, a Scots-Irish student at Glasgow University in 1704. [MUG#181]

BRISBANE, JOHN, a burgess of Bangor, County Down, 25 November 1612. [CSPIre#Carte pp.62/117]

BROWN, GAVEN, soldier of Colonel Bayly's Company in February 1648. [HMC.Ormonde.II.70]

BROWN, JAMES, master and merchant of the ....of Donaghadie at the port of Irvine on 28 August 1669. [NAS.E72.12.1]

BROWN, JAMES, a Scots-Irish student at Glasgow University in 1698. [MUG#165]

BROWN, JOHN, a burgess of Bangor, County Down, 25 November 1612. [CSPIre#Carte pp.62/117]

BROWN, JOHN, of Neale, Mayo, was admitted as a baronet of Nova Scotia on 29 September 1628. [NAS.BNS#59]

BROWN, JOHN, master of the Crystal of Donaghadie arrived in Irvine from Belfast on 24 June 1669. [NAS.E72.12.1]

BROWN, JOHN, master of the Mayflower of Donagadie at Port Patrick on 27 June 1684. [NAS.E72.20.10]

BROWN, SAMUEL, from Ireland, in Penningham in 1712. [Penningham KSR:13.8.1712]

BROWN, THOMAS, master of the Elizabeth of Portavadie arrived in the Clyde in December 1695 from Belfast. [NAS.E72.19.23]

BROWN, THOMAS, "a poor English traveller from Ireland", in Dumfries, 1699. [NAS.CH2.537.15.1/262]

BROWN, WILLIAM, a Scots-Irish student at Glasgow University in 1700. [MUG#169]

BROWNLEE, JOHN, a merchant from Clonish, Ireland, who was captured by the Turks when returning from Malaga, Spain, in 1685, father of Margaret. [RPCS.XII.308]

BRUCE, THOMAS, a clergyman in Taboyne, diocese of Clogher, 1614. [CSPIre#1614/920]

BRUCE, WILLIAM, in Tullyhogue, County Tyrone, 1610. [Tullyhogue Muster Roll]

BRUSS, JOHN, in Omagh, 1666. [Hearth Money Roll]

BRYAN, JOHN, a Scots-Irish student at Glasgow University in 1699. [MUG#167]

BUCHANAN, DAVID, a Lieutenant at Longford, 25 December 1678, also in 1680. [HMC.Ormonde#II, 216, 222]

BUCHANAN, JAMES, Captain of the Earl of Dunbarton's Regiment at Kinsale in April 1679. [HMC.Ormonde.II.219]

BUCHANAN, JOHN, was murdered by Lord Mayo during the rebellion, subsequently his children petitioned the Council, 24 January 1656. [CSP.Domestic, Interregnum I/92/38]

BUCHANAN, JOHN, a merchant in Dublin, 1684. [NAS.RH1.2.797/2]

BUCHANAN, JOHN, a defender at the Siege of Derry, 29 July 1689. [WDSD]

BUCHANAN, WILLIAM, a burgess of Newton Ards, County Down, 17 January 1612. [CSPIre.Carte pp62/84]

BUCHANAN, WILLIAM, was appointed Dean of Killala and Achonry on 1 February 1628. [CPR#436]

BURN, JOHN, son of the late Thomas Burn, a farmer in 'Colrain', was apprenticed to Edward Robison a barber and periwig-maker in Edinburgh on 1 April 1713. [REA]

BURNETT, JAMES, a Scots-Irish student at Glasgow University in 1703. [MUG#178]

BURNETT, JOHN, of Ballyleek, County Monaghan, 14 July 1631. [CPR#583]

BURNSIDE, DAVID, master of the Elizabeth of Londonderry arrived in the Clyde from Belfast in July 1696. [NAS.E72.19.23]

BURNSIDE, WILLIAM, master of the Vine of Londonderry arrived in Glasgow on 14 May 1689 from Londonderry. [NAS.E72.19.14]

BYRES, ROBERT, master of the Bettie of Belfast, from Rotterdam to Aberdeen in 1707. [ACA.APB.2]

CAIRNOCHAN, JOHN, from Ireland, in Penningham in 1705, also 1709. [Penningham KSR, 8.8.1705; 23.2.1709]

CALDWELL, CHARLES, Lieutenant Colonel of the Irish Dragoons in 1693. [DAL.III.300]

CALDWELL, HUGH, son of Sir James Caldwell of Castle Caldwell, County Fermanagh, possibly a Captain of the Inniskilling Dragoons in 1689. [DAL.III.34]

CALDWELL, JAMES, 1634-1717. [PRONI#D429/119]

CALDWELL, JOHN, master of the St Andrew of Belfast at Port Glasgow on 5 February 1691. [NAS.E72.19.21]

CALDWELL, ROBERT, an Ensign of the Inniskilling Regiment of Foot, in 1691. [DAL.III.206]

CALHOUN, HEW, master of the Sarah of Coleraine, arrived in Glasgow on 6 October 1684 from Coleraine. [NAS.E72.19.9]

CALHOUNE, ALEXANDER, Chaplain to Mountjoy's Regiment of Foot in 1695. [DAL.IV.109]

CALLENDAR, WILLIAM, a burgess of Newton Ards, County Down, 17 January 1612. [CSPIre.Carte pp62/84]

CAMPBELL, AGNES, daughter of Archibald Campbell, fourth Earl of Argyll, widow of James McDonnell, and wife of Turlough Lynagh O'Neill, 1581. [CalSPIre.LXXXVII]

CAMPBELL, ALEXANDER, husbandman of Island Magee, County Antrim, see deposition dated 14 May 1652. [ISC.I.274]

CAMPBELL, ALEXANDER, Lieutenant of the Earl of Dunbarton's Regiment at Kinsale in April 1679. [HMC.Ormonde.II.219]

CAMPBELL, ARCHIBALD, a prisoner in Kilkenny, December 1647. [CSP.Domestic. Interegnum. E26/123]

CAMPBELL, COLIN, a burgess of Rathmullen, County Donegal, 18 November 1612. [CSPIre.Carte pp62/87]

CAMPBELL, DONALD, a prisoner in Kilkenny, December 1647. [CSP.Domestic. Interegnum. E26/123]

CAMPBELL, DOUGALL, in Belfast, 1699, son of Alexander Campbell a merchant in Edinburgh. [NAS.RH15.9.14/67]

CAMPBELL, DUNCAN, a prisoner in Kilkenny, December 1647. [CSP.Domestic. Interegnum. E26/123]

CAMPBELL, HUGH, son of Josias Campbell in Ireland, was apprenticed to Samuel Hay, a wright in Edinburgh, on 15 November 1682. [REA]

CAMPBELL, JAMES, Lieutenant of the Earl of Dunbarton's Regiment at Kinsale in April 1679. [HMC.Ormonde.II.219]

CAMPBELL, JAMES, an Ensign of the Inniskilling Regiment of Foot, in 1691. [DAL.III.206]

CAMPBELL, JAMES, a Scots-Irish student at Glasgow University in 1700. [MUG#170]

CAMPBELL, JOHN, a defender at the Siege of Derry, 29 July 1689. [WDSD]

CAMPBELL, JOHN, a Scots-Irish student at Glasgow University in 1698. [MUG#165]

CAMPBELL, JOHN, a Scots-Irish student at Glasgow University in 1701. [MUG#171]

CAMPBELL, JOHN, from Ireland, in Penningham in 1712. [Penningham KSR:7.5.1712]

CAMPBELL, JOSHUA, a Lieutenant of the Londonderry Regiment of Foot in 1689; was appointed a Captain of Mitchelburne's Regiment of Foot on 12 March 1692. [DAL.III.83/272]

CAMPBELL, Reverend LACHLAN, transferred from Campbeltown, Argyll, to Capel Street, Dublin, during 1707. [NAS.CH1/2/27/157]

CAMPBELL, MABEL, daughter of the late Hew Campbell the Customs Collector at Donaghadie, married John Hamilton the minister of South West Kirk in Edinburgh, at Currie, Midlothian, on 29 June 1698. [Currie Marriage Register]

CAMPBELL, MARY, from Ireland, in Penningham in 1710. [Penningham KSR:8.2.1710]

CAMPBELL, PATRICK, master of the Fish-hook of Donaghadie arrived in Glasgow on 13 May 1689 from Dublin. [NAS.E72.19.14]

CAMPBELL, WILLIAM, son of James Campbell of Cassall in Ireland, a witness 19 June 1618. [NAS.Argyll Sasines#1/44]

CAMPBELL, WILLIAM, at Ballichering, Ireland, 1620. [NAS.Argyll Sasine #1/137]

CAMPBELL, WILLIAM, master of the Gift of Glenarme arrived in Glasgow on 18 May 1666 from Coleraine. [NAS.E72.10.2]

CAMPBELL, WILLIAM, a defender at the Siege of Derry, 29 July 1689. [WDSD]

CAMPSIE, HENRY, a defender at the Siege of Derry, 29 July 1689. [WDSD]

CANING, THOMAS, a passenger on the Jean of Irvine arrived in Ayr on 9 September 1673 from Londonderry. [NAS.E72.3.3]

CANTLEY, PATRICK, a merchant burgess of Elgin, Morayshire, settled in Ireland by 1707. [ACA.APB.2]

CAREMONT, JAMES, from Ireland, 1689. [NAS.CN2.537.15.1/15-66]

CARGILL, JOHN, a Scots-Irish student at Glasgow University in 1701. [MUG#172]

CARMICHAEL, WILLIAM, soldier of Colonel Bayly's Company in February 1648. [HMC.Ormonde.II.70]

CARR, FRANCIS, Tullyhogue, County Tyrone, 1610. [Tullyhogue Muster Roll]

CARR, GEORGE, with a sword and pike, Tullyhogue, County Tyrone, 1610. [Tullyhogue Muster Roll]

CARR, GEORGE, in Tullyhogue, County Tyrone, 1610. [Tullyhogue Muster Roll]

CARR, HENRY, Ensign of the Earl of Dunbarton's Regiment at Kinsale in April 1679. [HMC.Ormonde.II.219]

CARR, JAMES, a defender at the Siege of Derry, 29 July 1689. [WDSD]

CARR, JOHN, Lieutenant of the Earl of Dunbarton's Regiment at Kinsale in April 1679. [HMC.Ormonde.II.219]

CARR, ROBERT, Lieutenant of the Earl of Dunbarton's Regiment at Kinsale in April 1679. [HMC.Ormonde.II.219]

CARRUTHERS, ROBERT, master of the Janet of Donaghadie at Port Patrick on 4 October 1681; master of the Mayflower of Donagahdie at Port Patrick on 7 June 1682; master of the

Jonas of Donaghadie at Port Patrick on 3 August 1682. [NAS.E72.20.4/5]

CARRUTHERS, WILLIAM, from Ireland, 1689. [NAS.CH2.1284.15.1/24-27]

CARSON, CHARLES, Lieutenant of the Earl of Dunbarton's Regiment at Kinsale in April 1679. [HMC.Ormonde.II.219]

CARSWALL, JOHN, master and merchant of the John of Holywood arrived in the Clyde from Belfast in June 1691. [NAS.E72.19.21]

CARTER, HENRY, a citizen of Coleraine, with a wife and two children, 1690. [RPCS.XV.385]

CATHCART, JAMES, in Ulster by 1627. [CPR#233]

CATHCART, MALCOLM, a Captain of the Inniskilling Regiment of Foot, at Dundalk in October 1689. [DAL.III.122]

CEMMICK, PETER, a carpenter from Washford, a prisoner in Greenock, to be exchanged for a Scot in Irish hands, 1642. [RPCS.VII.339]

CHALMERS, DAVID, a Captain of the Londonderry Regiment of Foot in 1689. [DAL.III.83]

CHAPMAN, JAMES, master of the Joan of Belfast arrived in Port Glasgow on 22 December 1681 from Belfast. [NAS.E72.19.5]

CHARTERS, ROBERT, Lieutenant of the Earl of Dunbarton's Regiment at Kinsale in April 1679. [HMC.Ormonde.II.219]

CHARTERS, WILLIAM, from Ireland, 1689. [NAS.CH2.1284.15.1/22-24]

CHEARNSIDE, GEORGE, killed by rebels at Tully Castle, County Fermanagh, on 25 December 1641. See Patrick Hume's deposition. [ISC.I.215]

CHICHESTER, ARTHUR, Earl of Donegal, Viscount Chichester of Carrickfergus, Lord Baron of Belfast, was admitted as a

burgess and guilds-brother of Glasgow on 5 May 1701.
[GBR]

CHICHESTER, Reverend EDWARD, was admitted as a burgess
and guilds-brother of Glasgow on 5 May 1701. [GBR]

CHRISTIAN, THOMAS, a seaman from Waterford, a prisoner in
Greenock, to be exchanged for a Scot in Irish hands, 1642.
[RPCS.VII.339]

CLARK, THOMAS, a Scots-Irish student at Glasgow University in
1699. [MUG#166]

CLELAND, JAMES, formerly provost of Bangour, County Down,
was admitted as a burgess of Irvine, Ayrshire, on 13 May
1667. [MRBI#217]

CLERK, ROBERT, a merchant from Ayr, was robbed by Irish
rebels when bound for the west of Ireland, 1616.
[NAS.RH9.17.32]

CLERKE, DAVID, Lieutenant of the Earl of Dunbarton's
Regiment at Kinsale in April 1679. [HMC.Ormonde.II.219]

COBHAM, THOMAS, a minister from Ireland in Dumfries-shire
1689. [NAS.CH2.1284.2/39-48]

COCHRAN, ADAM, merchant of the James and Robert of Belfast,
arrived in the Clyde in March 1696 from Belfast.
[NAS.E72.19.23]

COCHRAN, Sir BRICE, a petitioner, 1657. [CSP.Domestic,
Interregnum. I/77/445,704]

COCHRAN, DAVID, a passenger on the Providence of Saltcoats
arrived in Ayr on 13 August 1678 from Dublin.
[NAS.E72.3.4]

COCHRAN, Lieutenant Colonel H., in Antrim, 1645.
[CSPIre.#CCLX]; a petitioner, 1658. [CSP.Domestic.
Interregmum, 1/78/445]

COCHRAN, JAMES, a Scots-Irish student at Glasgow University in 1702. [MUG#175]

COCHRAN, JOHN, a defender at the Siege of Derry, 29 July 1689. [WDSD]

COCHRAN, ROBERT, a Scots-Irish student at Glasgow University in 1701. [MUG#172]

COCHRANE, Sir WILLIAM, of Cowdoun, to Ireland in 1645. [NAS.PA7.3.102]

COCKBURN, GEORGE, Ensign of the Earl of Dunbarton's Regiment at Kinsale in April 1679. [HMC.Ormonde.II.219]

COCKBURN, ..., a Captain Lieutenant of the Londonderry Regiment of Foot in 1689. [DAL.III.83]

COLDEN, ROBERT, a minister in Ireland who fled to Scotland in 1642. [SLT#148]

COLQUHOUN, ROBERT, was granted letters patent of denization and 1000 acres in Portlogh, County Donegal, - the manor of Corkagh – on 14 July 1630. [CPR#538]

COLTRANE, JOHN, master of the <u>Ann of Portaferry</u> arrived in Glasgow on 25 January 1666. [NAS.E72.10.1]

COLVILL, ALEXANDER, was appointed as Precentor of the church of St Saviour of Connor on 8 August 1628. [CPR#328]

COLVILL, Sir ROBERT, in Ireland, 1691. [RPCS.XVI.281]

COLVILLE, ALEXANDER, 1620-1676. [PRONI#D562/1]

COLVILLE, ALEXANDER, in Carrickfergus, 1658. [CSPIre#CCLXXXVII/96]

COLVILLE, ALEXANDER, 1700-1777. [PRONI.T699/2]

COLVILLE, JAMES, a burgess of Bangor, County Down, 25 November 1612. [CSPIre#Carte pp.62/117]

COMBE, JOHN, a Scots-Irish student at Glasgow University in 1704. [MUG#180]

COMBLIN, GILBERT, with children, refugees from Ireland, 1689. [NAS.CH2.537.15.1/14]

COMERFORT, PATRICK, son of William Comerfort, a merchant from Waterford, a prisoner in Greenock, to be exchanged for a Scot in Irish hands, 1642. [RPCS.VII.339]

COMYN, ROBERT, Strabane Muster Roll of 1630. [PRONI#T808/15164]

CONNER, WILLIAM, a Scots-Irish student at Glasgow University in 1703. [MUG#177]

CONYNGHAM, ADAM, Lieutenant of the Earl of Dunbarton's Regiment at Kinsale in April 1679. [HMC.Ormonde.II.219]

CONYNGHAM, Sir ALBERT, son of Alexander Conyngham the Dean of Raphoe, a Captain of the Inniskilling Dragoons in 1689, killed at Colooney near Sligo on 11 September 1691. [DAL.III.35]

CONYNGHAM, ALEXANDER, Lieutenant of the Earl of Dunbarton's Regiment at Kinsale in April 1679. [HMC.Ormonde.II.219]

CONYNGHAM, HENRY, son of Sir Albert Conyngham, Captain of Mountjoy's Regiment of Foot, Colonel of the Inniskilling Dragoons in 1691, was killed in Spain during January 1706. [DAL.III.183/300]

CONYNGHAM, Lieutenant Colonel JOHN, in Antrim, 1645. [CSPIre.#CCLX]

CONYNGHAM, WILLIAM, Strabane Muster Roll of 1630. [PRONI#T808/15164]

COPRAN, THOMAS, a merchant from Dublin, was attacked and robbed in northern Ireland by Scottish pirates during 1584. [RPCS.IV.1586]

CORDINER, WILLIAM, a Scots-Irish student at Glasgow University in 1699. [MUG#167]

CORMACK, WILLIAM, surgeon of the Inniskilling Regiment of Foot in 1693. [DAL.III.336]

CORNWALL, JOSIAS, a Scots-Irish student at Glasgow University in 1699. [MUG#166]

CORRY, JOHN, a Captain of the Inniskilling Regiment of Foot, at Dundalk in October 1689. [DAL.III.122]

CORSBIE, Sir PEIRS, a member of the Privy Council of Ireland, , was admitted as a baronet of Nova Scotia on 24 April 1630. [NAS.BNS#74]

CORSBIE, WALTER, of Corsbie Park, County Wicklow, was admitted as a baronet of Nova Scotia on 24 April 1630. [NAS.BNS#59]

CORSON, JOHN, master of the James of Belfast arrived in Port Patrick on 13 September 1672 from Ireland. [NAS.E72.20.4]

COWAN, DANIEL, master of the Kathrine of Larne arrived in Glasgow on 1 October 1672. [MAS.E72.10.3]

COWAN, DONALD, master of the Swallow of Carrickfergus which arrived in the Clyde in April 1691 from Dublin. [NAS.E72.19.21]

COWAN, ROBERT, a Scots-Irish student at Glasgow University in 1700. [MUG#169]

CRAFORD, GEORGE, master of the Content of Strangford arrived in Glasgow in January 1666 from Dublin. [NAS.E72.10.1]

CRAFORD, JOHN, died 1701. [Ardstraw gravestone]

CRAG, JOHN, master and merchant of the Providence of Portaferry from Irvine to Ireland on 29 July 1681. [NAS.E72.12.3]

CRAGG, CHARLES, a Scots-Irish student at Glasgow University in 1699. [MUG#167]

CRAIG, GABRIEL, master of the Elizabeth of Belfast arrived in the Clyde from Belfast in November 1695. [NAS.E72.19.23]

CRAIG, Sir JAMES, was granted the manor of Fontesland, County Kildare, on 9 June 1627. [CPR#252]

CRAIG, ROBERT, in Aghabane, 8 March 1689. [NAS.GD406.1.3409]

CRAIG, WILLIAM, master of the Good Intention of Knock from Irvine to Carrickfergus on 18 July 1682. [NAS.E72.12.6]

CRAIGHEAD, ROBERT, a Scots-Irish student at Glasgow University in 1700. [MUG#169]

CRANSTON, JOHN, of Achhinie, Ireland, 1726. [NAS.Argyll Sheriff Court Book #IX, 4.7.1730]

CRAWFORD, ANDREW, 1696-1726. [PRONI#T101/2/362, 345]

CRAWFORD, DAVID, son of Owen Crawford in Donegal, accompanied the Earl of Tyrconnell to France but returned to Killibeg, Donegal, on 29 April 1610. [CSPIre#CCXXIX]

CRAWFORD, DAVID, from Ireland, in Penningham in 1709. [Penningham KSR:10.8.1709]

CRAWFORD, JAMES, master of the George of Strangford arrived in Glasgow on 18 January 1670 from Dublin. [NAS.E72.10.2]

CRAWFORD, JOHN, a burgess of Ayr, to Lough Swilly in 1575. [CalSPIre.vol.L]

CRAWFORD, JOHN, a merchant on the Nightingale of Donaghadie arrived in Ayr on 19 November 1677 from Dunnacaig. [NAS/E72.3.4]

CRAWFORD, OWEN, and wife, parents of David Crawford, residents of Donegal, 1610. [CSPIre.CCXXIX]

CRAWFORD, PATRICK, Captain of Foot at the Lyffer on 5 November 1608. [CSPIre#CCXXV]

CRAWFORD, PATRICK, Provost of Bangor, County Down, 25 November 1612. [CSPIre#Carte pp.62/117]

CRAWFORD, ROBERT, in Tullyhogue, County Tyrone, 1610. [Tullyhogue Muster Roll]

CRAWFORD, ROBERT, in Cullaghy, Drumra parish, Omagh, 1666. [Hearth Money Roll]

CRAWFORD, ROBERT, master of the George of Coleraine arrived in the Clyde from Coleraine on 5 November 1696. [NAS.E72.19.23]

CRAWFORD, THOMAS, 1670. [PRONI#T780/5-15]

CRAWFORD, WILLIAM, merchant of the Anna of Larne arrived at Larne on 5 January 1669 from Larne. [NAS.E72.12.1]

CRAWFORD, WILLIAM, master of the Phoeneix of Coleraine from Port Glasgow to Londonderry in April 1690. [NAS.E72.19.19]

CREA, JOHN, master of the Mayflower of Holywood at Loch Ryan on 29 August 1685. [NAS.E72.20.12]

CREICHTON, JOHN, in Ireland, heir to John Creichton of Achlean, brother of Sir Robert Creichton alias Murray of Gladmoor, 13 February 1724. [ECA.Moses.175/6906]

CREIGHTON, ABRAHAM, Colonel of the Inniskilling Regiment of Foot in 1691. [DAL.III.217]

CREIGHTON, DAVID, son of Colonel Abraham Creighton, defended his home Crum Castle against King James's forces in 1689, a Captain in Brudenell's Regiment of Foot in 1702, etc, , was appointed Governor of the Fort and Castle of Ross in County Kerry on 23 February 1701. [DAL.IV.264]

CREIGHTON, GEORGE, cleric of Virginia, County Cavan, 1643. [ISC.II.388][Harleian mss#5999]

CREIGHTON, GEORGE, Captain of Foot in Limerick, 22 March 1675, there 25 December 1678, also in July 1680. [HMC.Ormonde#II, 204, 218, 224]

CREIGHTON, JAMES, in County Leitrim, 1631. [CPR#586]

CREIGHTON, JOHN, a drummer, Tullyhogue, County Tyrone, 1610. [Tullyhogue Muster Roll]

CREIGHTON, JOHN, in Tullyhogue, County Tyrone, 1610. [Tullyhogue Muster Roll]

CREIGHTON, ROBERT, rector of Boghagh, 1631. [CPR#593]

CRICHTON, ALEXANDER, late of Glaslogh, County Monaghan, deposition dated February 1641. [ISC.I.189]

CRICHTON, ROBERT, a merchant traveller, from Loch Larne, Ireland, to Saltcoats, Ayrshire, in 1686. [RPCS.XII.378]

CRIGHTON, JAMES, a Scots-Irish student at Glasgow University in 1701. [MUG#171]

CRIGHTON, THOMAS, a Scots-Irish student at Glasgow University in 1701. [MUG#171]

CRISWALL, JOHN, master of the John of Hollywood arrived in Glasgow on 5 October 1686 from Belfast. [NAS.E72.19.12]

CRISWELL, EDWARD, master of the Rose of Coleraine arrive din Glasgow on 29 January 1689. [NAS.E72.19.14]

CROFFORD, ANDREW, a landowner in the parish of Dunnaghy, barony of Killenway, 1660. [MA#466]

CROOKSHANK, JOHN, in Londonderry, 1719. [NAS.NRAS#104/2/419]

CROOKSHANK, WILLIAM, chamberlain of Londonderry, 1689. [NAS.NRAS#104/2/175]

CROSBIE, ARCHIBALD, possibly a Captain of the Inniskilling Regiment of Horse in 1689. [DAL.III.27]

CRUICKSHANK, ANDREW, master of the John of Londonderry arrived in Port Glasgow on 17 September 1691 from Virginia. [NAS.E72.19.21]

CRUICKSHANK, THOMAS, master of the Margaret of Donaghadie at Port Patrick on 7 October 1682. [NAS.E72.20.7]

CUILLEN, ANDREW, from Ireland, a prisoner in Edinburgh Tolbooth in 1685. [RPCS.XI.295]

CUNNINGHAM, ADAM, master of the Anna of Coleraine at the port of Irvine on 9 November 1668; master and merchant of the Agnes of Coleraine at the port of Irvine on 10 May 1669; arrived in Irvine on 6 August 1669 from Coleraine. [NAS.E72.12.1]

CUNNINGHAM, ALEXANDER, a burgess of Killileagh, 17 November 1612. [CSPIre#Carte pp62/110]

CUNNINGHAM, ALEXANDER, Prebend of Invernally, County Donegal, was appointed as Dean of Raphoe on 9 December 1629. [CPR#523]

CUNNINGHAM, DAVID, of Heurt, leased 240 acres in County of Coleraine, from Sir Robert McClellane of Bomby in 1614. [PRONI#T640]

CUNNINGHAM, GEORGE, in 1627 he became a founder burgess of St Johnstown, County Longford. [CPR#250]

CUNNINGHAM, Sir JAMES, in County Donegal, husband of Lady Catherine, parents of George and two daughters, 1627. [CPR#266]

CUNNINGHAM, JAMES, was granted letters patent of denization and granted the manor of Fort Cunningham in County Donegal on 29 May 1629. [CPR#453]

CUNNINGHAM, JAMES, a defender at the Siege of Derry, 29 July 1689. [WDSD]

CUNNINGHAM, JOHN, brother of Sir James Cunningham, in County Donegal, 1627. [CPR#267]

CUNNINGHAM, JOHN, a defender at the Siege of Derry, 29 July 1689. [WDSD]; a Lieutenant of the Londonderry Regiment of Foot in 1689. [DAL.III.83]

CUNNINGHAM, JOHN, from Ireland, in Penningham, 1713. [Penningham KSR, 20.5.1713]

CUNNINGHAM, JOSEPH, a Lieutenant of the Londonderry Regiment of Foot in 1689. [DAL.III.83]

CUNNINGHAM, MICHAEL, a defender at the Siege of Derry, 29 July 1689. [WDSD]; Captain of the Londonderry Regiment of Foot in 1689. [DAL.III.83]

CUNNINGHAM, MURDO, Captain of the Inniskilling Regiment of Foot, 1693. [DAL.III.336]

CUNNINGHAM, SAMUEL, a Cornet of the Inniskilling Dragoons in 1689. [DAL.III.35]

CUNNINGHAM, WILLIAM, a burgess of Strabane, County Tyrone, 25 November 1612. [CSPIre#Carte.pp62/117]

CUNNINGHAM, WILLIAM, Articlare, County Londonderry, 1635. [NAS.RH15.91.61]

CUNNINGHAM, Lieutenant Colonel WILLIAM, a landowner in the parish of Dunnaghy, barony of Killenway, 1660. [MA#466]

CUNNINGHAM, WILLIAM, a Scots-Irish student at Glasgow University in 1702. [MUG#175]

CURRIE, ARCHIBALD, a Scots-Irish student at Glasgow University in 1703. [MUG#177]

CUTHBERTSON, JAMES, a 'sea-merchant' in Ireland, who was killed at the siege of Londonderry, leaving a widow Catherine Bruce, and their four children, 1690. [RPCS.XV.385]

DALLAY, ROBERT, in Dublin, and his son Alexander Dallay, 23 October 1696. [NAS.GD97.576]

DARROCH, DUGALD, a Scots-Irish student at Glasgow University in 1704. [MUG#180]

DARROCH, JOHN, a Scots-Irish student at Glasgow University in 1700. [MUG#169]

DAVIDSON, ALEXANDER, master of the Jane and Mary of Belfast at the port of Irvine in February 1716, [NAS.E508.10.6]

DAVIDSON, JOHN, master of the Happy Return of Portaferry arrived in Ayr during April 1673. [NAS.E72.3.3]

DAVIE, JAMES, master of the Elizabeth of Larne arrived in Glasgow on 24 July 1666 from Carrickfergus. [NAS.E72.10.1]

DAVIE, JOSEPH, a merchant in Londonderry, was admitted as a burgess and guilds-brother of Glasgow on 6 June 1715. [GBR]

DAVIES, NATHANIEL, master of the Fullwood ketch of Belfast bound for Belfast from Port Glasgow on 5 August 1682. [NAS.E72.19.6]

DAVIS, HENRY, mayor of Carrickfergus, 1689. [RPCS.XVI.310]

DAVISON, WALTER, master and merchant of the Friends Adventure of Londonderry from Port Glasgow to Londonderry on 26 November 1689. [NAS.E72.19.17]

DEAN, ANDREW, in Drumfeldy, County Antrim, 1698. [NAS.NRAS#2522/CA4/1/34]

DEAN, ANDREW, a Scots-Irish student at Glasgow University in 1701. [MUG#171]

DEAN, JOHN, son of Andrew Dean, in Drumfeldy, County Antrim, 1706. [NAS.NRAS#2522/CA3/18]

DEAN, WILLIAM, master and merchant of the Margaret of Larne arrived in Irvine in April 1669 from Larne. [NAS.E72.12.1]

DICK, WILLIAM, Lieutenant Colonel of the Scots Army, in Coleraine pre 1647. [APS.VI.i.756]

DICK, WILLIAM, a Scots-Irish student at Glasgow University in 1705. [MUG#182]

DICKSON, ARCHIBALD, an Irish student at Glasgow University in 1699. [MUG#167]

DICKSON, WILLIAM, 1723. [PRONI#T580/57]

DONALDSON, JOHN, a proprietor in the parish of Carncastle, barony of Glencarn, 1641. [MA#457]

DONALDSON, JOHN, in Carrickfergus, 1658. [CSPIre#CCLXXXVII/96]

DONALDSON, JOHN, a landowner in the parish of Glenarme, and in the parish of Layde, barony of Glenarme, in 1660. [MA#466]

DONNALLIE, JOHN, an Irish merchant who arrived in Ayr in September 1672 on board the Unity of Ayr from Barbados, [AA.B6.18.4]

DOOKE, ALEXANDER, master of the Providence of Coleraine arrived in Glasgow on 30 January 1686 from Dublin. [NAS.E72.19.12]

DOUGALL, ANDREW, a burgess of Rathmullen, County Donegal, 18 November 1612. [CSPIre.Carte pp62/87]

DOUGLAS, ANDREW, master of the Sarah of Ballintoy from Glasgow to Coleraine on 8 July 1686. [NAS.E72.19.13]

DOUGLAS, ANNE, Duchess of Hamilton, 1632-1716.
[PRONI#T2247]

DOUGLAS, Sir ARCHIBALD, married Lady Elinor widow of Sir
John Davies an undertaker in County Fermanagh, by 1632.
[CSPIre#CCLXX/25]

DOUGLAS, Sir ARCHIBALD, Captain of the Earl of Dunbarton's
Regiment at Kinsale in April 1679. [HMC.Ormonde.II.219]

DOUGLAS, ROBERT, Captain of the Earl of Dunbarton's
Regiment at Kinsale in April 1679. [HMC.Ormonde.II.219]

DOUGLAS, WILLIAM, a gentleman in Connaught, 4 June 1659.
[CSPIre#CCLXXXVII/172]

DOUGLAS, Sir WILLIAM, Captain of the Earl of Dunbarton's
Regiment at Kinsale in April 1679. [HMC.Ormonde.II.219]

DOUGLAS, Mrs, from Ireland, in Penningham in 1712.
[Penningham KSR:13.2.1712]

DOUNIE, JOHN, master of the Marie of Portaferry arrived in
Glasgow on 7 June 1686 from Dublin. [NAS.E72.19.12]

DRUMMOND, DAVID, of Mylnab, born around 1612, eldest son
of James Drummond of Mylnab and his wife Marion Murray,
educated at St Andrews University, minister of Crieff,
Perthshire, from 1635 to 1649, moved to Ireland, Episcopal
rector of Omagh by 1668, killed at Clogher in 1676, husband
of Isabel, daughter of David Sibbald a Baillie of Perth, and
widow of William Drummond a burgess of Perth, parents of
John and David. [Fasti.4.265]

DRUMMOND, MALCOLM, was granted letters patent of
denization and granted the manor of Castle Drummond in
County Tyrone on 23 May 1629. [CPR#453]

DUDAILL, STEVEN, in Dundalk, was admitted as a burgess and
guilds-brother of Glasgow on 1 January 1596. [GBR]

DUFF, WILLIAM, master of the William of Leith, arrived in Cork
during February 1609 from Cadiz. [CSPIre#CCXXVIII]

DUFF, WILLIAM, master of the Jane of Carrickfergus arrived in Glasgow on 30 October 1686 from Carrickfergus. [NAS.E72.19.12]

DUN, JOHN, from Ireland, in Minnigaff parish on 18 December 1720. [Minnigaff Kirk Session Records, 15.1.1721]

DUNBAR, ALEXANDER, a burgess of Inniskilling, 12 October 1612. [CSPIre.Carte pp62/106]

DUNBAR, ANDREW, a Lieutenant of the Londonderry Regiment of Foot in 1689. [DAL.III.83]

DUNBAR, Sir JOHN, 1692. [PRONI#T1089/61]

DUNBAR, MARGARET, from Ireland to Dumfries in 1690. [NAS.CH2.537.15.1/34]

DUNBAR, PHILIP, a defender at the Siege of Derry, 29 July 1689. [WDSD]

DUNBAR, ROBERT, was appointed to the prebend of Rasarhan in Connor Cathedral, 25 November 1628. [CPR#427]

DUNBAR, THOMAS, from Ireland, in Penningham in 1712. [Penningham KSR:13.8.1712]

DUNBAR, WILLIAM, a burgess of Killileagh, 17 November 1612. [CSPIre#Carte pp62/110]

DUNCAN, DAVID, merchant of the Salmon of Belfast arrived in Port Glasgow on 4 November 1695. [NAS.E72.19.23]

DUNCAN, JAMES, master and merchant of the Margaret of Larne arrived in Irvine on 30 September 1669 from Larne. [NAS.E72.12.1]

DUNCAN, THOMAS, a skipper from Kirkcaldy, imprisoned in Ireland, 1647. [APS,VI.i.718]

DUNDAS, JAMES, chaunter of Moray, was appointed Bishop of Down and Connor on 23 February 1612. [CSPIre]

DUNDAS, JAMES, Ensign of the Earl of Dunbarton's Regiment at Kinsale in April 1679. [HMC.Ormonde.II.219]

DUNLOP, ALEXANDER, a Scots-Irish student at Glasgow University in 1703. [MUG#177]

DUNLOP, BRICE, was granted 100 acres at Gortconny, and on 18 September 1623 another 210 acres, died 4 April 1674, [MA#440]

DUNLOP, DAVID, master and merchant of the ......of Larne at the port of Irvine on 9 June 1669. [NAS.E72.12.1]

DUNLOP, DAVID, a Scots-Irish student at Glasgow University in 1702. [MUG#175]

DUNLOP, JOHN, a Scots-Irish student at Glasgow University in 1699. [MUG#167]

DUNLOP, SAMUEL, (1), a Scots-Irish student at Glasgow University in 1699. [MUG#167]

DUNLOP, SAMUEL, (2), a Scots-Irish student at Glasgow University in 1699. [MUG#167]

DUNLOP, WILLIAM, a Scots-Irish student at Glasgow University in 1700. [MUG#169]

DUNN, JOHN, master of the Mayflower of Glenarme arrived in Glasgow from Coleraine on 25 September 1670. [NAS.E72.10.2]

DUNWIDDY, RINGAN, in Achanamirll, Drumra parish, Omagh, 1666. [Hearth Money Roll]

DUYNE, JOHN, master of the Goodspeed of Glenarme arrived in Port Glasgow from Dublin on 4 September 1683. [NAS.E72.19.8]

DYER, WILLIAM, to Ireland in 1714. [Penningham KSR, 30.5.1714]

DYKES, JAMES, a Scots-Irish student at Glasgow University in 1705. [MUG#182]

ECCLES, DANIEL, a student from Ireland at Glasgow University in 1664. [MUG#115]

ECCLES, ROBERT, in Omagh, 1666. [Hearth Money Roll]

ECHLIN, ROBERT, third son of Robert Echlin of Ardquin, County Down, a Captain of Colonel John Cunningham's Regiment of Foot, Lieutenant Colonel of the Inniskilling Dragoons in 1689, Colonel of the Regiment from 1691 to 1716. [DAL.III.35/183]

EDGAR, JOHN, from Ireland, in Penningham in 1710. [Penningham KSR:10.5.1710]

EDMONSTONE, ANNA, sister of William Edmonstone of Braid Island, County Antrim, and Alexander Houston, second son of William Houston of Cottreoche, marriage contract, dated 10 September 1625. [NAS.GD97.Sec.1/381]

EDMONSTONE, ANNA HELENA, of Broadisland, County Anrtim, widow of Archibald Edmonstone, sister and heir of Walter Scott the younger, deceased, and to Colonel Walter Scott, senior, deceased, 23 October 1696. [NAS.GD97.576]

EDMONSTONE, ARCHIBALD, witness, Braid Island, County Antrim, 10 September 1625. [NAS.GD97.Sec.1/381]

EDMONDSTONE, ARCHIBALD, of Duntreath, settled in Ballycarry, County Antrim, during 1609, [HS#587/8]; 1631. [CPR#578]

EDMONSTONE, ARCHIBALD, son of the late William Edmonstone of Braidland, County Antrim, versus Sir Claud Hamilton of Craigleith, 27 February 1627. [NAS.GD97.Sec.1/385]

EDMONSTONE, ARCHIBALD, of Broadisland, County Antrim, and Anna Helena Adair, widow of William Adair of Ballymanoch or Kinhilt, marriage contract, 17 April 1666. [NAS.GD97.Sec.1/501]

EDMONSTONE, JAMES, witness, Braid Island, County Antrim, 10 September 1625. [NAS.GD97.Sec.1/381]

EDMONSTONE, JAMES, of Ballinbanstra, was appointed by his cousin Archibald Edmonstone of Braidyland, as steward of the Manor of Dallouch, 29 October 1630. [NAS.GD97.Sec.1/399]

EDMONSTONE, JAMES, of Brodiland, County Antrim, authorised to buy arms in Scotland for the use of soldiers in Ireland, 6 January 1642. [RPCS.VII.177]

EDMONSTONE, ROBERT, a burgess of Charlemont, County Armagh, 20 April 1613. [CSPIre#Carte pp 62/79]

EDMONSTONE, ROBERT, witness, 29 October 1630. [NAS.GD97.Sec.1/399]

EDMONSTONE, WILLIAM, if Braid Island, County Antrim, leased lands of Ballytemple, Balleybley, and others, to Janet, wife of Robert, Bishop of Down, and John Echlin of the College of St Andrews, 6 September 1622. [NAS.GD97.Sec.1/376]

EDMONT, DANIEL, a merchant traveller from Dunlewar, County Liew (sic), Ireland, later in Loch Larne, with his wife Jean, to Saltcoats, Ayrshire, in 1686. [RPCS.XII.378]

EDWARD, JAMES, master of the Elizabeth of Larne from Port Glasgow on 26 February 1681 bound for Belfast; arrived in Ayr on 8 November 1681 from Ireland; from Port Glasgow to Dublin on 5 April 1683 [NAS.E72.3.1/8/9]

EDWARD, THOMAS, master of the Merchant of Larne from Irvine to Belfast on 13 January 1682. [NAS.E72.12.6]

ELLIOT, ARCHIBALD, with a sword, Tulluhogue, County Tyrone, 1610. [Tulluhogue Muster Roll]

ELLIOT, JOHN, with a sword and snaphance, Tulluhogue, County Tyrone, 1610. [Tulluhogue Muster Roll]

ELLIOT, ROBERT, (1) in Tullyhogue, County Tyrone, 1610. [Tullyhogue Muster Roll]

ELLIOT, ROBERT, (2) in Tullyhogue, County Tyrone, 1610. [Tullyhogue Muster Roll]

ELLIOT, WILLIAM, with a sword and snaphance, Tulluhogue, County Tyrone, 1610. [Tulluhogue Muster Roll]

ELLIOT, WILLIAM, (1) in Tullyhogue, County Tyrone, 1610. [Tullyhogue Muster Roll]

ELLIOT, WILLIAM, (2), in Tullyhogue, County Tyrone, 1610. [Tullyhogue Muster Roll]

ELLIOT, WILLIAM, a Scots-Irish student at Glasgow University in 1701. [MUG#171]

ENRIKEN, DANIEL, an Irishman who was captured during 1641 in Kirkcudbright and imprisoned in Edinburgh Tolbooth. [RPCS.VII.210/221]

ERSKINE, ARCHIBALD, was appointed rector and vicar of Toalcarbott and Aghemallen, in the Diocese of Clogher on 24 September 1627; rector of Deenish, County Fermanagh, was granted lands in County Fermanagh, on 29 February 1631. [CPR#276/592]

ERWIN, GEORGE, a Scots-Irish student at Glasgow University in 1703. [MUG#177]

ERWIN, JANE, in Ballyluggan, County Tyrone, 1641. [ISC.I.288]

FAIRLIE, ROBERT, of Fairlie in the parish of Largs, Ayrshire, was granted the lands of Lisconnan on 14 February 1617. [MA#440]

FAIRLY, DAVID, a Scots-Irish student at Glasgow University in 1701. [MUG#171]

FALCONER, ALEXANDER, a sergeant of Colonel Anstruther's regiment, to Ireland in 1724. [NAS.CH2.537.1/214]

SCOTS-IRISH LINKS

FALCONER, JOHN, master of the James of Strangford arrived in Glasgow on 3 September 1672 from Dublin. [NAS.E72.10.3]

FEARIE, THOMAS, master of the New Venture of Glenarme from Irvine to Ireland on 5 November 1680. [NAS.E72.12.3]

FENTON, WILLIAM, a proprietor in the parish of Carncastle, barony of Glencarn, 1641. [MA#457]

FERGUSON, ANDREW, in Tullyhogue, County Tyrone, 1610. [Tullyhogue Muster Roll]

FERGUSON, Sergeant Major FINDON, in Antrim, 1645. [CSPIre.#CCLX]

FERGUSON, SAMUEL, a Lieutenant of the Londonderry Regiment of Foot in 1689. [DAL.III.83]

FERRIER, WILLIAM, master of the Martin of Belfast from Port Glasgow to Belfast in October 1689. [NAS.E72.19.15]

FERRY, JOHN, a passenger on the Marian of Island McGee arrived in Ayr on 2 August 1673 from Ireland. [NAS.E72.3.3]

FINLAY, ALEXANDER, soldier of Colonel Bayly's Company in February 1648. [HMC.Ormonde.II.69]

FINLAY, JOHN, snr, soldier of Colonel Bayly's Company in February 1648. [HMC.Ormonde.II.69]

FINLAY, JOHN, jr, soldier of Colonel Bayly's Company in February 1648. [HMC.Ormonde.II.69]

FINLAY, ROBERT, soldier of Colonel Bayly's Company in February 1648. [HMC.Ormonde.II.69]

FISHER, EDWARD, from Ireland to Dumfries in 1690. [NAS.CH2.537.15.1/29]

FISHER, HUGH, a Scots-Irish student at Glasgow University in 1700. [MUG#169]

FISHER, JOHN, master of the Ann of Coleraine arrived in Glasgow on 29 June 1666 from Coleraine. [NAS.E72.10.1]

FLEMING, GEORGE, 1620-1676. [PRONI#T729/2/26]

FLEMING, JAMES, 1620-1676. [PRONI#T729/2/26]

FLEMING, JAMES, a defender at the Siege of Derry, 29 July 1689. [WDSD]

FLEMING, JAMES, chaplain of the Royal Regiment of Dragoons of Ireland in 1696. [DAL.IV.119]

FLEMING, JAMES, was appointed an Ensign of Mountjoy's Regiment of Foot on 1 April 1697, 1701. [DAL.IV.191/259]

FLEMING, Sir JOHN, 1685-1703. [PRONI#T848/22]

FLEMING, JOHN, Lieutenant of Mountjoy's Regiment of Foot, 1695, 1701. [DAL.IV.109/259]

FLEMING, RICHARD, a defender at the Siege of Derry, 29 July 1689. [WDSD]

FLEMING, ROBERT, Lieutenant of the Earl of Donegal's Regiment of Foot in 1701. [DAL.IV.257]

FLOOD, JOHN, an Irishman who was captured in Kirkcudbright during 1641 and imprisoned in Edinburgh Tolbooth. [RPCS.VII.210/221]

FLYNN, JOHN, master of the Bonadventure of Killork arrived in Glasgow on 31 January 1689 from Strangford. [NAS.E72.19.14]

FORBES, ALEXANDER, 10th Baron Forbes, 1672. [PRONI#D562/38]

FORBES, ARTHUR, Earl of Granard, 1623-1695. [PRONI#D638/11/17]

FORBES, Captain ARTHUR, in 1627 he became a founder burgess of St Johnstown, County Longford. [CPR#250]; of

Castle Forbes, County Longford, was admitted as a baronet of Nova Scotia on 29 September 1628. [NAS.BNS#59]

FORBES, ARTHUR, in 1627 he became a founder burgess of St Johnstown, County Longford. [CPR#55/567/250]

FORBES, Sir ARTHUR, Colonel of Horse quartered at Mollingar, 27 August 1670, and in Dublin 17 September 1672. [HMC.Ormonde#II, 197, 199, 202]

FORBES, ARTHUR, a Cornet quartered in Dublin in August 1677, also in July 1680. [HMC.Ormonde#II, 207, 223]

FORBES, ROBERT, Cornet of the Regiment of Guards at Dublin in July 1680. [HMC.Ormonde.II.223]

FORGIE, SAMUEL, a Scots-Irish student at Glasgow University in 1703. [MUG#177]

FORREST, GEORGE, master of the William and Robert of Belfast at Port Glasgow in May 1689. [NAS.E72.19.14]

FORRET, JAMES, was granted lands in County Longford on 28 May 1625. [CPR#55]

FORSYTH, JOHN, an Ensign of the Londonderry Regiment of Foot in 1689. [DAL.III.83]

FOSTER, JOHN, master of the Helen of Strangford, arrived in Glasgow on 10 July 1666 from Dublin. [NAS.E72.10.1]

FRASER, SIMON, 11th Lord Lovat, 1667-1747. [PRONI#D2470]

FRAZER, ALEXANDER, Captain at Carrickfergus, 25 December 1678. [HMC.Ormonde#II, 214]

FRISSELL, ALEXANDER, master of the Isobel of Glenarme at Port Patrick on 19 July 1682. [NAS.E72.20.7]

FRISSELL, JAMES, a Scots-Irish student at Glasgow University in 1703. [MUG#177]

FULLARTON, FERGUS, maltman in the parish of Billy, see deposition dated 1 March 1652. [ISC.I.239]

FULLARTON, RALPH, a defender at the Siege of Derry, 29 July 1689. [WDSD]

FULTON, ALEXANDER, was appointed a Lieutenant of Creighton's Regiment of Foot in 1694. [DAL.IV.41]

FULTON, JAMES, a workman from Antrim, was accused of bigamy having married Agnes Currie in Dumfries but with a wife and family in Ireland, 1692. [NAS.CH2.1284.2/147]

FULTON, Mrs NICOLA, wife of James Fulton, Aughidowny, parish of Dunboe, see deposition dated at Coleraine on 22 March 1652. [ISC.I.342]

GAIRDNER, JOHN, a merchant in Armagh, was admitted as a burgess and guildsbrother of Ayr on 31 March 1726. [Ayr Burgess Roll]

GALBRAITH, HUGH, in Belligallie, was admitted a burgess and guildsbrother of Ayr on 3 July 1676. [Ayr Burgess Roll]

GALBRAITH, HUGH, probably from Tyrone, possibly a Captain of the Inniskilling Dragoons in 1689, promoted to Major on 20 July 1695. [DAL.III.34]

GALBRAITH, JAMES, merchant of the Phoenix of Coleraine from Port Glasgow to Londonderry in April 1690. [NAS.E72.19.19]

GALBRAITH, JAMES, a Scots-Irish student at Glasgow University in 1700. [MUG#169]

GALBREATH, Captain ARTHUR, in Dublin, 1726. [Argyll Sheriff Court Book, #VIII, 23.3.1726], and in 1730. [Argyll Sheriff Court Book, #IX, 4.7.1730]

GALBREATH, Sergeant Major JAMES, in Antrim, 1645. [CSPIre.#CCLX]

GALRY, JEAN, from Ireland, in Penningham in 1710.
[Penningham KSR:8.11.1710]

GALRY, JOHN, in Ireland, 1711. [Penninghame Kirk Session
Records, 8.11.1711]

GALT, JOHN, in Ireland, 1659, possibly linked with Robert Galt a
miller in Irvine, Ayrshire. [MRBI#88]

GARLAND, THOMAS, from Ireland, in Penningham in 1709.
[Penningham KSR:10.8.1709]

GARNER, RICHARD, master of the Isobell of Belfast arrived in
Port Glasgow on 7 October 1682 from Barbados.
[NAS.E72.19.5]

GEALLY, JOHN, in Kerereoch, Ireland, brother of the late Ninian
Geally in Rothesay, 1687. [Rothesay Town Council Records,
6.4.1687]

GETTY, SAMUEL, a Scots-Irish student at Glasgow University in
1704. [MUG#180]

GIB, JAMES, provost, Strabane Muster Roll of 1630.
[PRONI#T808/15164]

GIBB, JAMES, a gentleman in County Longford, 1626. [CPR#151]

GIBSON, EDMUND, 1669-1748. [PRONI#MIC310/T659/107]

GIBSON, GEORGE, a burgess of Newton Ards, County Down, 17
January 1612. [CSPIre.Carte pp62/84]

GIBSON, JOHN and ROBIN, leased lands of Ballibrie and
Ballimainstra, Grayabbeylands, from William Edmonstone of
Braichland on 16 October 1623. [NAS.GD97.Sec.1/378]

GIBSON, ROBERT, a burgess of Clogher, 12 December 1612.
[CSPIre.Carte pp62/77]

GILCHRIST, JOHN, merchant of the St Andrew of Belfast at Port
Glasgow on 5 February 1691. [NAS.E72.19.21]

GILL, ALEXANDER, 1636-1677. [PRONI#T970]

GILLES, JOHN, master and merchant of the Betty of Carrickfergus from Irvine to Ireland on 21 March 1681. [NAS.E72.12.3]

GILMOR, JOHN, master of the Joan of Belfast bound from Port Glasgow to Belfast on 7 March 1682. [NAS.E72.19.6]

GILMOR, Major, an Irishman who was captured in Kirkcudbright and imprisoned in Edinburgh Tolbooth during 1641. [RPCS.VII.210/221]

GILMORE, JOHN, formerly of Gabroch, Ayrshire, then in Ireland by 1633. [NAS.NRAS#3957/7, 10]

GIVAN, JOHN, in Omagh, 1666. [Hearth Money Roll]

GLEDSTANES, JAMES, a defender at the Siege of Derry, 29 July 1689. [WDSD]

GLEN, WILLIAM, a Scots-Irish student at Glasgow University in 1701. [MUG#172]

GLENDENNING, JAMES, in Tullyhogue, County Tyrone, 1610. [Tullyhogue Muster Roll]

GLENDENNING, JOHN, with a sword and pike, Tullyhogue, County Tyrone, 1610. [Tullyhogue Muster Roll]

GLENDENNING, PATRICK, in Tullyhogue, County Tyrone, 1610. [Tullyhogue Muster Roll]

GLENDENNING, ROBERT, a gentleman in County Longford, 1626. [CPR#151]

GLENDY, JOHN, in Culnagard, Drumra parish, Omagh, 1666. [Hearth Money Roll]

GORDON, AGNES, married a soldier in Lismagartae, Ireland, in April 1715, in Penningham by April 1716. [Penningham KSR, 29.4.1716]

GORDON, ALEXANDER, a burgess of Newton Ards, County Down, 17 January 1612. [CSPIre.Carte pp62/84]

GORDON, Captain GEORGE, of Ballylany, County Antrim, died by 22 November 1690, husband of Margaret. [Irish Bills of Exchequer, 22.11.1690]

GORDON, JAMES, in Bangor, see deposition dated 3 May 1653. [ISC.I.284]

GORDON, JAMES, from Ireland, in Penningham in 1710. [Penningham KSR:8.2.1710]

GORDON, JOAN, from Ireland, in Kingarth, 1694. [Kingarth Kirk Session Records, 9.9.1694]

GORDON, JOAN, widow of James Falconer late in Lisgarden, Ireland, before 1707. [ACA.APB.2]

GORDON, JOHN, cousin of Richard Fynglas, 1608. [CSPIre#CCXXV/263]

GORDON, Sir JOHN, 1580-1656. [PRONI#T520]

GORDON, JOSEPH, a defender at the Siege of Derry, 29 July 1689. [WDSD]

GORDON, NICHOLAS, uncle of Richard Fynglas, 1608. [CSPIre#CCXXV/263]

GORDON, ROBERT, son and heir of Sir Robert Gordon, in County Longford, 1626. [CPR#151]

GORDON, ROBERT, Lieutenant of the Earl of Dunbarton's Regiment at Kinsale in April 1679. [HMC.Ormonde.II.219]

GORDON, ROBERT, a Scots-Irish student at Glasgow University in 1703. [MUG#177]

GORDON, THOMAS, from Ireland, in Penningham in 1710. [Penningham KSR:10.5.1710]

GOSS, ROBERT, master of the Marigold of Belfast from Port Glasgow to Madeira in December 1690. [NAS.E72.19.22]

GOWDIE, JOHN, son of Gilbert Gowdie in Bellycosting, Ireland, was apprenticed to Patrick Hunter, a cordiner in Edinburgh, on 22 September 1680. [REA]

GRAHAM, Major ARTHUR, storekeeper at Eniskillen, County Fermanagh, 1667, [NAS.RH15.91.61]; quartermaster at Lisburn, 25 December 1678, also in July 1680. [HMC.Ormonde#II, 214, 227]

GRAHAM, ARTHUR, Cornet to Colonel Robert Echlin of the Inniskilling Dragoons, 30 November 1693. [DAL.III.299]

GRAHAM, CHRISTIAN, widow of James Murray minister of Ochir in Ireland who was killed, along with his eldest son, by rebels in 1641, fled with her eleven children to Scotland by 1642. [SLT#150]

GRAHAM, FERGUS, a pensioner, ca.1609. [CSPIre#CCXXVII]

GRAHAM, FRANCIS, quartermaster of the Life Guards in Ireland, 22 March 1675. [HMC.Ormonde.II/203]

GRAHAM, GEORGE, Lieutenant of the Earl of Dunbarton's Regiment at Kinsale in April 1679. [HMC.Ormonde.II.219]

GRAHAM, HANS, Cornet of Horse in the North of Ireland, 22 March 1675. [HMC.Ormonde#II,203]

GRAHAM, JAMES, Lieutenant of the Earl of Dunbarton's Regiment at Kinsale in April 1679. [HMC.Ormonde.II.219]

GRAHAM, JAMES, a defender at the Siege of Derry, 29 July 1689. [WDSD]

GRAHAM, Sir RICHARD, was granted lands in Queen's County and in King's County on 25 May 1603; constable of the Fort of Old Court, Connaught, 1610. [CSPIre#CCXIII/66; CCXXIX/128]

GRAHAM, RICHARD, master of the Mary of Holywood arrived in Glasgow on 22 November 1666 from Holywood. [NAS.E72.10.1]

GRAHAM, SIMON, soldier of Colonel Bayly's Company in February 1648. [HMC.Ormonde.II.69]

GRAHAM, THOMAS, Ensign at Fenae, Connaught, 25 December 1678. [HMC.Ormonde#II, 216]

GRAHAM, WILLIAM, a husbandman on Island Magee, 1641, see deposition dared 1 June 1653. [ISC.I.267]

GRANGER, ROBERT, and his wife Kathren Hill, settled in Dunnalong, County Tyrone, in 1610. died around 1630. [Grange gravestone, County Tyrone]

GRANT, JAMES, Ensign of the Earl of Dunbarton's Regiment at Kinsale in April 1679. [HMC.Ormonde.II.219]

GRANT, RICHARD, in County Waterford, in 1627. [CPR#225]

GRAVAT, GEORGE, merchant in Carrickfergus, was admitted as a burgess and freeman of Rothesay on 6 December 1665. [Rothesay Town Council Records, 6.12.1665]

GRAY, ARCHIBALD, master of the Margaret of Donaghadie at Port Patrick on 19 February 1672; master of the Isobell of Donaghadie from Port Patrick to London on 22 August 1672. [NAS.E72.20.2/4]

GRAY, ARCHIBALD, from Rothesay to Ireland in 1711. [Rothesay KSR, 4.3.1711]

GRAY, DAVID, of Billy, County Antrim, see deposition dated 1 March 1652. [ISC.I.248]

GREENWAY, EDWARD, an Anglo-Irish student at Glasgow University in 1701. [MUG#171]

GREIG, ANDREW, master of the Snow of Belfast, which arrived in Loch Ryan, Scotland, from Virginia 1689. [RPCS.13.538];

master of the Swan of Donaghadee arrived at Ayr in August 1690 from Virginia. [AA.B6.18.4/373]

GRIERSON, CONSTANTIA, 1706-1733. [PRONI#t393/4]

GRIERSON, JOHN, formerly in Nether Keir, Dumfries-shire, then in County Monaghan, by 8 January 1639. [CLC#223]

GRIFFITH, ANNA, widow of Thomas Murray the minister of Killisea, Ireland, who was killed by rebels, fled to Scotland by 1642. [SLT#166]

GRIGSON, ANDREW, a defender at the Siege of Derry, 29 July 1689. [WDSD]

GUIN, WILLIAM, master of the Recovery of Donaghadie arrived in the Clyde in October 1695 from Londonderry. [NAS.E72.19.23]

GUTHRIE, JAMES, of Ballygriffin, a yeoman, was murdered by rebels in 1641. [ISC.II.41]

GUTHRIE, JAMES, master of the Providence of Balliwalter from Glasgow to Dublin on 2 March 1667. [NAS.E72.10.1]

GUTHRIE, JAMES, merchant of the Prosperity of Belfast at Port Glasgow in January 1691. [NAS.E72.19.21]

HACKETT, JAMES, Major of the Earl of Dunbarton's Regiment at Kinsale in April 1679. [HMC.Ormonde.II.219]

HAGER, JANET, from Ireland, was buried in Greyfriars, Edinburgh, on 29 September 1689. [Greyfriars Burial Register]

HAIR, WILLIAM, a Scots-Irish student at Glasgow University in 1699. [MUG#166]

HAIRSTONE, JOHN, in Knockshinnoch, Irongray parish, was accused of adultery and fled to Ireland in 1693. [NAS.CH2.1284.2/175]

HALL, JAMES, a Scots-Irish student at Glasgow University in 1702. [MUG#174]

HALL, THOMAS, in Carrickfergus, 1649; a minister in Ireland, a receipt dated 1657. [GA#276] [ECA.Moses.186/77/35]

HALLIDAY, SAMUEL, a minister from Ireland, who preached in the parishes of Dunscore and Dryfesdale, Dumfries-shire, in 1689. [NAS.CH2.1.84.2/40-151]

HAMILL, HUGH, a defender at the Siege of Derry, 29 July 1689. [WDSD]

HAMILL, HUGH, Colonel of a Londonderry or Inniskilling Regiment in 1690; Captain of Mountjoy's Regiment of Foot, 1694. [DAL.III.168/391]

HAMILL, JOHN, son of the late John Hamill a clerk in Strabane, was apprenticed to John Merston a skinner in Edinburgh on 8 May 1689. [Edinburgh Register of Apprentices]

HAMILL, ROBERT, in Ballymoney parish, see deposition dated 4 March 1652. [ISC.I.234]

HAMILTON, Sir ALEXANDER, 1625-1633. [PRONI#T580/50]

HAMILTON, ALEXANDER, second Baron of Dalzell, 1692. [PRONI#T640]

HAMILTON, ALEXANDER, Captain of Brudenell's Regiment of Foot on the Irish Establishment, 1701. [DAL.IV.255]

HAMILTON, ANDREW, a defender at the Siege of Derry, 29 July 1689. [WDSD]

HAMILTON, ANDREW, Captain of the Inniskilling Regiment of Foot, 1691. [DAL.III.206]

HAMILTON, ARCHIBALD, 1580-1659. [PRONI#T808/6246]

HAMILTON, ARCHIBALD, son of Malcolm Hamilton the Lord Archbishop of Cashel, granted tithes of lands in County Fermanagh on 17 July 1626. [CPR#609]

HAMILTON, ARCHIBALD, Bishop of Killala and Ardconragh, was appointed Archbishop of Cashel and Bishop of Emly on 29 April 1630. [CPR#537]

HAMILTON, ARCHIBALD, Major of Mountjoy's Regiment of Foot, 1694, 1701. [DAL.III.391/259]

HAMILTON, ARCHIBALD, an Irish student at Glasgow University in 1699. [MUG#167]

HAMILTON, ARTHUR, a defender at the Siege of Derry, 29 July 1689. [WDSD]

HAMILTON. CHARLES, Captain of Foot in HM Army in Ireland 18 November 1667, quartered in Cavan 20 April 1668, and at Finae 27 August 1670; Captain of the Life Guards, 22 March 1675.. [HMC.Ormonde#II, 194, 195, 197, 202]

HAMILTON, CLAUDE, Captain of a Regiment of Foot quartered in Borresowle/Borrisoule, County Mayo, 20 April 1668, also on 27 August 1670. [HMC.Ormonde#II, 196, 198]

HAMILTON, DANIEL, merchant of the Catherine of Donaghadie at the port of Kirkcudbright in 1673. [NAS.E72.6.2]

HAMILTON, EDWARD, rector of Donacavagh, 1631. [CPR#593]

HAMILTON, Mrs ELIZABETH, wife of Patrick Hamilton of Ballygrangeghe, received letters patent of denization on 5 July 1631. [CPR#59]

HAMILTON, FRANCIS, of Killach, County Down, was admitted as a baronet of Nova Scotia on 29 September 1628. [NAS.BNS#59]

HAMILTON, FRANCIS, Lieutenant at Carlingford, 25 December 1678, also in 1680. [HMC.Ormonde.#II, 214, 222]

HAMILTON, FRANCIS, Captain of the Ulster Horse at Killishandra in August 1680. [HMC.Ormonde.II.226]

HAMILTON, FREDERICK, a Cornet quartered in Ballygaully in August 1677. [HMC.Ormonde#II, 207]

HAMILTON, FREDERICK, a Captain quartered in Killishandra 25 December 1678, and in Londonderry in July 1680. [HMC.Ormonde#II, 215, 226]

HAMILTON, FREDERICK, Lieutenant of the Earl of Dunbarton's Regiment at Kinsale in April 1679. [HMC.Ormonde.II.219]

HAMILTON, FREDERICK, was appointed Captain of the Royal Regiment of Foot of Ireland on 6 June 1701. [DAL.IV.249]

HAMILTON, GEORGE, a petitioner, pre 1632. [CSPIre#CCLXX/28]

HAMILTON, GEORGE, Captain of a Regiment of Foot quartered in Galway, 20 April 1668. [HMC.Ormonde#II, 196]

HAMILTON, Lord GEORGE, Captain of the Earl of Dunbarton's Regiment at Kinsale in April 1679. [HMC.Ormonde.II.219]; Colonel of the Inniskilling Regiment of Foot in 1691. [DAL.III.206]

HAMILTON, ..., a merchant in Londonderry, 1689. [PES.I.16]

HAMILTON, GUSTAVUS, quartermaster at Drogheda, 25 December 1677, there 25 December 1678, possibly quartered in Coloony in 1680. [HMC.Ormonde#II, 214, 225]

HAMILTON, GUSTAVUS, Captain of a Regiment of Foot, in Londonderry in July 1680. [HMC.Ormonde.II.226]

HAMILTON, Sir HANS, Captain of Foot in HM Army in Ireland 18 November 1667, quartered in Carlingford 20 April 1668; Lieutenant Colonel of a Troop of Horse quartered at Charlemont 27 August 1670; at Carlingford, 25 December 1678; also in July 1680. [HMC.Ormonde#II, 194, 195, 198, 214, 222]

HAMILTON, HUGH, a burgess of Killileagh, 17 November 1612. [CSPIre#Carte pp62/110]

HAMILTON, HUGH, a burgess of Bangor, County Down, 25 November 1612. [CSPIre#Carte pp.62/117]

HAMILTON, HUGH, Baron Hamilton of Deserf, 1669. [PRONI.DOD#257]

HAMILTON, HUGH, merchant on the Christian of Carrickfergus arrived in Ayr on 18 June 1678 from Dunaveady; merchant on the Betty of Belfast arrived in Ayr on 26 September 1681 from Belfast. [NAS.E72.3.4/7]

HAMILTON, JAMES, in County Down, 1606. [CPR#232]

HAMILTON, JAMES, a burgess of Killileagh, 17 November 1612. [CSPIre#Carte pp62/110]

HAMILTON, Sir JAMES, a burgess of Strabane, County Tyrone, 25 November 1612. [CSPIre#Carte.pp62/117]

HAMILTON, JAMES, a burgess of Clogher, 12 December 1612. [CSPIre.Carte pp62/77]

HAMILTON, JAMES, a leaseholder of lands near Ballymoney, 28 February 1621. [MA#439]

HAMILTON, JAMES, witness, Braid Island, County Antrim, 10 September 1625. [NAS.GD97.Sec.1/381]

HAMILTON, JAMES, a debtor in Ireland of Lord Antrim in 1638. [MA#476]

HAMILTON, JAMES, a passenger in the Katherine of Larne arrived in Ayr on 20 August 1673 from Ireland. [NAS.E72.3.3]

HAMILTON, JAMES, a Scots-Irish student at Glasgow University in 1701. [MUG#171]

HAMILTON, JAMES, a Scots-Irish student at Glasgow University in 1702. [MUG#174]

HAMILTON, JAMES, a merchant in Belfast, who was admitted as a burgess of Glasgow on 6 September 1707. [GBR]

HAMILTON, JOHN, Provost of Strabane, County Tyrone, 25 November 1612. [CSPIre#Carte.pp62/117]

HAMILTON, JOHN, a burgess of Strabane, County Tyrone, 25 November 1612. [CSPIre#Carte.pp62/117]

HAMILTON, JOHN, was given letters patent of denization and granted lands in County Cavan and County Armagh on 29 July 1629. [CPR#478]

HAMILTON, JOHN, (1) a defender at the Siege of Derry, 29 July 1689. [WDSD]

HAMILTON, JOHN, (2) a defender at the Siege of Derry, 29 July 1689. [WDSD]

HAMILTON, JOHN, a Captain of the Londonderry Regiment of Foot in 1689; appointed Lieutenant Colonel of Mitchelburne's Regiment of Foot on 12 March 1692. [DAL.III.83/272]

HAMILTON, JOHN, master of the William of Londonderry from the Clyde to Londonderry in April 1690. [NAS.E72.19.19]

HAMILTON, JOHN, from Ireland, in Penningham in May 1707. [Penningham KSR, 27.5.1714]

HAMILTON, MALCOLM, Lord Archbishop of Cashel, 1626. [CPR#609][HMC, 14th Report, #79/80]

HAMILTON, MALCOLM, a Cornet of a Regiment of Foot at Ballygally in July 1680. [HMC.Ormonde.II.227]

HAMILTON, MALCOLM, Major of the Inniskilling Regiment of Foot in 1691. [DAL.III.217]

HAMILTON, MARGARET, daughter of Lieutenant Colonel William Hamilton in Ireland, and widow of the late Captain James Montgomery of Killicole, County Fermanagh, moved to Scotland by 1646. [SLT#196]

HAMILTON, MARGARET, from Ireland, in Penningham in February 1708. [Penningham KSR, 11.11.1707]

HAMILTON, PETER, a burgess of Killileagh, 17 November 1612. [CSPIre#Carte pp62/110]

HAMILTON, RICHARD, a Cornet of the Inniskilling Dragoons in 1689, was appointed a Lieutenant of the regiment in 1699. [DAL.III.35/221]

HAMILTON, ROBERT, a burgess of Strabane, County Tyrone, 25 November 1612. [CSPIre#Carte.pp62/117]

HAMILTON, ROBERT, was appointed vicar of Donnoghle in the Diocese of Cashel, etc., 22 May 1629. [CPR#444]

HAMILTON, ROBERT, Lieutenant of the Earl of Dunbarton's Regiment at Kinsale in April 1679. [HMC.Ormonde.II.219]

HAMILTON, ROBERT, a minister in Ireland, 1689. [NAS.CH2.1284.2/46]

HAMILTON, THOMAS, a burgess of Rathmullen, County Donegal, 18 November 1612. [CSPIre.Carte pp62/87]

HAMILTON, WILLIAM, Provost of Killileagh, 17 November 1612. [CSPIre#Carte pp62/110]

HAMILTON, WILLIAM, (1), a burgess of Bangor, County Down, 25 November 1612. [CSPIre#Carte pp.62/117]

HAMILTON, WILLIAM, (2), a burgess of Bangor, County Down, 25 November 1612. [CSPIre#Carte pp.62/117]

HAMILTON, Sir WILLIAM, was granted lands in County Tyrone – the manor of Ellistown – on 20 November 1629. [CPR#479]

HAMILTON, Lieutenant WILLIAM, in County Tyrone, 1636. [CSPIre.#CCLV]

HAMILTON, WILLIAM, in Omagh, 1666. [Hearth Money Roll]

HAMILTON, WILLIAM, a defender at the Siege of Derry, 29 July 1689. [WDSD]; a Lieutenant of the Londonderry Regiment of Foot in 1689. [DAL.III.83]

HAMILTON, WILLIAM, a Captain of the Inniskilling Dragoons in 1689. [DAL.III.35]

HAMILTON, WILLIAM, Ensign of Courthope's Regiment of Foot, 1695. [DAL.IV.108]

HAMILTON, WILLIAM, Major of the Earl of Donegal's Regiment of Foot in 1701. [DAL.IV.257]

HANNAGH, ANDREW, a Captain-Lieutenant of the Inniskilling Dragoons in 1689. [DAL.III.35]

HANNAY, Sir ROBERT, was granted towns and lands in County Dublin on 25 May 1643, [CSPIre.#CCLX];Captain of Foot in HM Army in Ireland 18 November 1667. [HMC.Ormonde#II, 194]

HAR, THOMAS, an Irish student at Glasgow University in 1698. [MUG#164]

HARPER, ANDREW, a passenger in the Ellen of Kintyre arrived in Ayr on 27 July 1673 from Ireland. [NAS.E72.3.3]

HARPER, JAMES, with a sword, Tullyhogue, County Tyrone, 1610. [Tullyhogue Muster Roll]

HARPER, JAMES, in Tullyhogue, County Tyrone, 1610. [Tullyhogue Muster Roll]

HARPER, JOHN, a refugee from Ireland, in Edinburgh 1650. [SLT#301]

HARRIS, THOMAS, a Scots-Irish student at Glasgow University in 1701. [MUG#171]

HARRISON, JOHN, master and merchant of the Joan of Belfast from the Clyde to Madeira in January 1691. [NAS.E72.19.22]

HARVIE, JOHN, a probationer minister at New Abbey, Dumfries-shire, who was called to Ireland in 1689. [NAS.CH2.1284.2/50-251]

HATTRIDGE, JOHN, of Dromore, Ireland, was admitted as a burgess and guilds-brother of Glasgow on 23 September 1713, [GBR]; 1728. [NAS.NRAS#631/4/bundle A903]

HAY, FRANCIS, 9th Earl of Errol, 1631. [PRONI#D929/HA12/F4/1/6]

HAY, GEORGE, Earl of Kinnoull, 1572-1634. [PRONI#D929/HA12/F4/1/6]

HAY, Sir JAMES, was granted Castlebar etc in County Longford in 1636. [CSPIre.#CCLV]

HAY, RICHARD AUGUSTINE, 1661-1736. [PRONI#D618/38]

HAY, WILLIAM, Ensign of the Earl of Dunbarton's Regiment at Kinsale in April 1679. [HMC.Ormonde.II.219]

HEIGATE, JAMES, was given letters patent of denization and granted lands in County Fermanagh -- the manor of Heigate -- on 26 August 1629. [CPR#478]

HENDERSON, DAVID, a burgess of Newton Ards, County Down, 17 January 1612. [CSPIre.Carte pp62/84]

HENDERSON, JAMES, a Scots-Irish student at Glasgow University in 1704. [MUG#180]

HENDERSON, WILLIAM, an Irish student at Glasgow University in 1702. [MUG#173]

HENDRIE, ANDREW, a burgess of Clogher, 12 December 1612. [CSPIre.Carte pp62/77]

HENDRIE, HUGH, master of the Elizabeth of Donaghadie arrived in the Clyde in October 1696 from Belfast. [NAS.E72.19.23]

HENERY, DAVID, a Scots-Irish student at Glasgow University in 1701. [MUG#172]

HERBERTSON, ALEXANDER, a wright and looking-glass maker in Glasgow, deserted his wife Marion Steuart and eloped with his servant Jean Brodie to Belfast before 1726. [NAS.CC8.5.3]

HERON, NINIAN, a gentleman in County Longford, 1626. [CPR#151]

HERRIES, JOHN, merchant of the Joan of Belfast from Port Glasgow to Madeira in January 1691. [NAS.E72.19.22]

HERRON, ALEXANDER, Quarter-master of the Londonderry or Inniskilling Regiment in 1690. [DAL.III.168]

HETHERINGTON, THOMAS, a burgess of Agher, County Tyrone, 6 April 1613. [CSPIre.Carte pp62/101]

HETHERINGTON, WILLIAM, a pensioner, ca.1609. [CSPIre#CCXXVII]

HEWAT, ARCHIBALD, master of the Friendship of Londonderry, from Port Glasgow to Londonderry on 6 December 1689. [NAS.E72.19.17]

HILL, JOHN, in Carrickfergus, 1641, see deposition dated 1 June 1653. [ISC.I.265]

HILL, JOHN, master of the Marie of Limnavadie arrived in Port Glasgow on 19 August 1682 from Coleraine. [NAS.E72.19.5]

HILLHOUSE, JAMES, a Scots-Irish student at Glasgow University in 1704. [MUG#180]

HINDMAN, JAMES, a Scots-Irish student at Glasgow University in 1702. [MUG#175]

HINDMAN, JOHN, merchant on the Friends Adventure of Londonderry at Port Glasgow in October 1689. [NAS.E72.19.15]

HODGES, ROBERT, Captain of the Earl of Dunbarton's Regiment at Kinsale in April 1679. [HMC.Ormonde.II.219]

HOGG, THOMAS, minister at Duncannon, County Fermanagh, from 1632 to 1641, fled, with his wife, two children, and two younger brothers, via Mincha Castle and Londonderry to Scotland by 1642. [SLT#131]

HOLLYDAY, SAMUEL, a Scots-Irish student at Glasgow University in 1701. [MUG#171]

HOLMES, GABRIEL, master of the Gabriel of Belfast arrived in Port Glasgow on 19 May 1682 from Belfast. [NAS.E72.19.5]

HOLMES, JAMES, master of the James of Belfast arrived in the Clyde from Dublin on 31 August 1691. [NAS.E72.19.21]

HOLMES, JOHN, a Scots-Irish student at Glasgow University in 1704. [MUG#180]

HOLMES, JOHN, master of the James of Donaghadee at the port of Kirkcudbright in September 1715, [NAS.E508.10.6]

HOOD, JAMES, master of the John of Balliwalter arrived in Glasgow on 8 October 1672 from Londonderry. [NAS.E72.10.3]

HOUSTON, CHARLES, adjutant of HM army in Ireland, August 1677. [HMC.Ormonde#II, 206]

HOUSTON, JANET, born in Ireland, daughter of Captain Alexander Houston who was killed by rebels at Aulra, fled, with her seven brothers and sisters, to Ayr, Scotland, by 1642. [SLT#143]

HOUSTON, JOHN OGG, in County Antrim, 1631. [CPR#578]

HOUSTON, JOHN, an Ensign at Mullingar, Connaught, 25 December 1678. [HMC.Ormonde#II, 216]

HOUSTON, ROBERT, a refugee from Ireland, in Edinburgh by 1644. [SLT#211]

HOUSTON, ROBERT, a Scots-Irish student at Glasgow University in 1705. [MUG#182]

HOUSTON, WILLIAM, in County Antrim, 1631. [CPR#578]

HOUSTON, Captain WILLIAM, a landowner in the parish of Dunnaghy, and in the parish of Maghrasharran, barony of Killenway, 1660. [MA#466]

HOUSTON, WILLIAM, a merchant in Belfast, was admitted as a burgess and guilds-brother of Glasgow on 9 February 1715. [GBR]

HOUSTON, ..., Lieutenant Colonel of the Londonderry Regiment of Foot in 1689. [DAL.III.83]

HUGGIN, ROBERT, master of the Beattie of Belfast at Port Patrick on 18 July 1681. [NAS.E72.20.6]

HUIT, WILLIAM, an elder of Killinchy parish, 1710. [Minnigaff Kirk Session Records, 20 November 1720]

HUME, Mrs DOROTHY, widow of Reverend George Hume, Tully, Dublin, 1707. [NAS.GD158.1136]

HUME, GEORGE, of Drumkese, in Ireland, 1623. [NAS.GD158.533]

HUME, GEORGE, Captain of the Earl of Dunbarton's Regiment at Kinsale in April 1679. [HMC.Ormonde.II.219]

HUME, GEORGE, born in Scotland, flaxen hair, trooper of the King's Guard of Horse from 1665, later in Ireland. [HMC.Ormonde.II.237]

HUME, GEORGE, quartermaster of Sir John Hume's troop of the Inniskilling Regiment of Horse in 1689, fought at the battle of Newtown Butler. [DAL.III.27]

HUME, JOHN, a defender at the Siege of Derry, 29 July 1689. [WDSD]

HUME. Sir JOHN, of Castle Hume, County Fermanagh, possibly a Captain of the Inniskilling Regiment of Horse in 1689. [DAL.III.27/28]

HUME, MARY, 1705. [PRONI#DA173/291]

HUME, Captain PATRICK, Tully Castle, County Fermanagh, in 1641, see deposition at Inniskillen dated 1 April 1654. [ISC.I.214]

HUME, PATRICK, from Ireland to Dumfries in 1690. [NAS.CH2.537.15.1/48]

HUNTER, JAMES, master of the Jonas of Donaghadie at Port Patrick on 2 June 1681. [NAS.E72.20.5]

HUNTER, JAMES, a Scots-Irish student at Glasgow University in 1705. [MUG#182]

HUNTER, JOHN, master and merchant of the New Venture of Glenarme at the port of Irvine on 25 May 1669. [NAS.E72.12.1]

HUNTER, JOHN, master of the Katherine of Londonderry at Port Glasgow in January 1691. [NAS.E72.19.21]

HUNTER, JOHN, a Scots-Irish student at Glasgow University in 1701. [MUG#172]

HUNTER, NATHANIEL, master of the Janet of Glenarme at Port Patrick on 30 April 1685. [NAS.E72.20.10]

HUNTER, PATRICK, master and merchant of the Janet of Glenarme from Irvine on 3 January 1681 bound for Ireland, also on 4 August 1681. [NAS.E72.12.3/5]

HUNTER, ROBERT, master of the Mayflower of Londonderry from Glasgow to Londonderry on 25 March 1672. [MAS.E72.10.3]

HUNTER, ROBERT, merchant on the Charlemont of Belfast arrived in Ayr on 18 June 1678. [NAS.E72.3.4]

INCH, THOMAS, merchant in Carrickfergus, was admitted as a burgess and freeman of Rothesay on 6 December 1665. [Rothesay Town Council Records, 6.12.1665]

INGLIS, JOHN, son of the late David Inglis of Claddieford in Ireland, was apprenticed to Sir James Murray of Deuchar a merchant in Edinburgh on 26 May 1647. [REA]

INGLIS, MARY, from Ireland to Dumfries in 1690. [NAS.CH2.537.15.1/40]

INNES, ALEXANDER, Lieutenant of the Earl of Dunbarton's Regiment at Kinsale in April 1679. [HMC.Ormonde.II.219]

INNES, ALEXANDER, son of Gilbert Innes a farmer in County Armagh, was apprenticed to David Gray, a hat-maker in Edinburgh, on 1 June 1687. [REA]

INNES, JOHN, master of the Archibald and Mary of Donaghadie arrived in Port Patrick on 25 May 1681; master of the Archibald of Donaghadie at Port Patrick on 7 July 1682. [NAS.E72.20.5/7]

INNES, ROBERT, Lieutenant of the Earl of Dunbarton's Regiment at Kinsale in April 1679. [HMC.Ormonde.II.219]

IRVINE, CHRISTOPHER, soldier of Lieutenant Colonel Robert Byron's Company of Foot in Drogheda, December 1642. [HMC.Ormonde.II.15]

IRVINE, Sir GERARD, of Castle Irvine, County Fermanagh, fought for Charles II at Worcester, possibly a Captain of the Inniskilling Regiment of Horse in 1689, died at Dundalk and buried there. [DAL.III.27/28]

IRVINE, JOHN, in Tullyhogue, County Tyrone, 1610. [Tullyhogue Muster Roll]

IRWYN, WILLIAM, a Captain of the Londonderry Regiment of Foot in 1689. [DAL.III.83]

JACK, ANDREW, a passenger on the Hopewell of Irvine arrived in Ayr on 9 September 1673 from Londonderry. [NAS.E72.3.3]

JACKSON, JAMES, master of the Vine of Londonderry arrived in the Clyde in October 1691 from Londonderry. [NAS.E72.19.21]

JACKSON, THOMAS, eldest son and heir to James Jackson a surgeon in Ballintriebeg, Ireland, late owner of Little Barron, Rothesay, 1666. [Rothesay Town Council Records, 13.2.1666]

JAMIESON, JOHN, master of the Margaret of Donaghadie arrived in Glasgow on 1 June 1666 from Carrickfergus. [NAS.E72.10.2]

JAMIESON, ROBERT, an alleged pirate from Ayr, was accused of attacking and robbing Thomas Copran, a merchant from Dublin, in northern Ireland during 1584. [RPCS.IV.1586]

JARDINE, JAMES, son of William Jardine in Coleraine, was apprenticed to John Leyne, a merchant in Edinburgh, on 21 November 1649. [REA]

JEFFES, ROBERT, a merchant burgess of Edinburgh, then in Birr, King's County, Ireland, disposed of property in Edinburgh to Thomas Porteous, a merchant burgess, and his wife Janet Wardroper, on 18 September 1667. [ECA.Moses.59/2624]

JOHNSON, JOHN, Ensign of the Earl of Dunbarton's Regiment at Kinsale in April 1679. [HMC.Ormonde.II.219]

JOHNSTON, ADAM, master of the Good Fortune of Donaghadie arrived in Port Patrick on 23 December 1680 from Donaghadie; also on 1 November 1681. [NAS.E72.20.5/7]

JOHNSTON, ANDREW, pardoned on 17 August 1614. [CSPIre.Docquet Book]

JOHNSTON, ANNA, daughter of the late David Johnston, merchant, petitioned the Burgh Council of Edinburgh for money to join her husband in Ireland around 1657. She was granted £5. [ECA.Moses.186/7/2]

JOHNSTON, Cornet ARCHIBALD, descended from the Johnstons of Loderhay in Annandale, Scotland, died in March 167-, husband of Margaret (Graham?). [Castledearg gravestone, County Tyrone]

JOHNSTON, CHARLES, an Ensign of the Londonderry Regiment of Foot in 1689. [DAL.III.83]

JOHNSTON, FRANCIS, from Ireland to Dumfries in 1690. [NAS.CH2.537.15.1/29]

JOHNSTON, GEORGE, an Ensign of the Inniskilling Regiment of Foot, in 1691; Lieutenant of Colonel Gustavus Hamilton's Regiment of Foot on 24 March 1692, appointed 1st Lieutenant of Colonel Luke Lillington's Regiment of Foot, 'designed for Jamaica', on 24 December 1694. [DAL.III.206/263]

JOHNSTON, GILBERT, a husbandman, late of Cashel, County Tipperaray, see deposition dated 20 February 1642. [ISC.II.40]

JOHNSTON, JAMES, a Lieutenant of the Inniskilling Regiment of Foot, at Dundalk in 1691. [DAL.III.206]

JOHNSTON, JOHN, a Captain of the Inniskilling Regiment of Foot, at Dundalk in October 1689. [DAL.III.122]

JOHNSTON, JOHN, and family, from Ireland to Dumfries in 1690. [NAS.CH2.537.15.1/27]

JOHNSTON, JOHN, Lieutenant of the Irish Dragoons, commissioned on 8 December 1692. [DAL.III.231]

JOHNSTON, JOSEPH, a defender at the Siege of Derry, 29 July 1689. [WDSD]

JOHNSTON, MARY, from Ireland to Dumfries in 1690. [NAS.CH2.537.15.1/35]

JOHNSTON, ROBERT, from Ireland, in Penningham in 1710. [Penningham KSR:23.8.1710]

JOHNSTON, THOMAS, a defender at the Siege of Derry, 29 July 1689. [WDSD]

JOHNSTON, Mrs, from Ireland to Dumfries in 1690.
[NAS.CH2.537.15.1/43]

JOHNSTONE, EDWARD, probably fifth son of Walter Johnstone
of Maulick, County Fermanagh, a Captain of the Inniskilling
Regiment of Foot at Dundalk in October 1689.
[DAL.III.121/206]

JORDAN, JOHN, a Welsh-Irish student at Glasgow University in
1699. [MUG#167]

JULIUS, MARGARET, in County Down, sister and heir of
Alexander Julius late of Leith, Scotland, 1633.
[CSPIre#CCLXX/45]

KEATING, JOHN, an Anglo-Irish student at Glasgow University
in 1702. [MUG#175]

KEBRIE, JAMES, a Scots-Irish student at Glasgow University in
1703. [MUG#178]

KEITH, Sergeant Major GEORGE, in Antrim, 1645.
[CSPIre.#CCLX]

KEITH, HEW, son of the late Alexander Keith of Betlechachane in
Ireland, was apprenticed to James Borthwick, surgeon in
Edinburgh, on 26 March 1656. [REA]

KELBURN, NINIAN, son of Adam Kelburn in Rothesay, to
Ireland in 1706. [Rothesay KSR, 26.12.1706]

KELLIE, JAMES, master of the Marie of Belfast, arrived in
Glasgow on 12 June 1684 from Belfast. [NAS.E72.19.9]

KELSO, HENRY, a debtor in Ireland of Lord Antrim in 1638.
[MA#476]

KELSO, JOHN, fled to Ireland from Kingarth to avoid censure in
1666. [Kingarth Kirk Session Records, 18.2.1666]

KELSO, JOHN, a passenger in the Ellen of Kintyre arrived in Ayr
on 27 July 1673 from Ireland. [NAS.E72.3.3]

KEMP, WILLIAM, a Scots-Irish student at Glasgow University in 1700. [MUG#169]

KENNA, JOHN, an Anglo-Irish student at Glasgow University in 1698. [MUG#165]

KENNEDY, ALEXANDER, whose father had been murdered in Scotland, was dismissed from custody on 18 January 1612. [CSPIre.Docquet Book]

KENNEDY, ANTHONY, of Balsaragh, Kirkoswald, Ayrshire, husband of Ann Moore, father of Walter, settled in Antrim in 1603, resided at Turnarobert near Armey, with lands near Bushmills, died in 1620. [MA#64]

KENNEDY, DAVID, a burgess of Newton Ards, County Down, 17 January 1612. [CSPIre.Carte pp62/84]

KENNEDY, DAVID, Lieutenant at Charlemont, 25 December 1678, in Coleraine by July 1680. [HMC.Ormonds.#II, 215, 226]

KENNEDY, JAMES, whose father had been murdered in Scotland, was dismissed from custody on 18 January 1612. [CSPIre.Docquet Book]

KENNEDY, JAMES, was appointed as schoolmaster of the Free School of Donegal on 11 December 1629. [CPR#490]

KENNEDY, JOHN, a burgess of Bangor, County Down, 25 November 1612. [CSPIre#Carte pp.62/117]

KENNEDY, JOHN, a proprietor in the parish of Derrykeche, barony of Carie, 1641. [MA#457]

KENNEDY, JOHN, a constable of Donaghadee in 1647. [CSPIre.#CCLXIII]

KENNEDY, JOHN, master of the Good Fortune of Donaghadie at Port Patrick on 19 October 1682. [NAS.E72.20.7]

KENNEDY, JOHN, a Scots-Irish student at Glasgow University in 1698. [MUG#165]

KENNEDY, ROBERT, was appointed Chief Chamberlain of the Exchequer on 2 May 1625; was granted the manor of Baltinglass on 10 March 1626; he surrendered the office of Registrar or Clerk of the Faculties in Dublin on 31 March 1628; the Chief Remembrancer of Ireland on 7 May 1628; was granted a house in Bridge Street, Dublin, and the lands of Ballymony, County Wicklow, on 6 October 1628. [CPR#74/192/326/334/391]

KENNEDY, THOMAS, in 1627 he became a founder burgess of St Johnstown, County Longford. [CPR#250]

KENNEDY, THOMAS, son of the late David Kennedy of Kilrenie in Ireland, was apprenticed to John McLurge, a merchant in Edinburgh, on 2 November 1655. [REA]

KENNEDY, THOMAS, born in Scotland, brown hair, trooper of the King's Guard of Horse from 1669, later in Ireland. [HMC.Ormonde.II.238]

KENNEDY, THOMAS, a Scots-Irish student at Glasgow University in 1699. [MUG#166]

KENNEDY, WALTER, born 1596, son of Anthony Kennedy of Balsaragh, Kirkoswald, Ayrshire, and his wife Ann Moore, settled in Antrim in 1603, married ..... Boyd, daughter of William Boyd of Dunluce. [MA#64]

KENNEDY, WILLIAM, late of Torinvogan, County Wicklow, father of James Kennedy, 1629. [CPR#512]

KENNEDY, ...a former Alderman of Dundalk, via Irvine to Edinburgh in 1689. [PES.II.78/79]

KER, JAMES, in Carrickfergus, 5 May 1649. [GA#277]

KERNES, ALEXANDER, the general agent for the Scottish undertakers in the precinct of Boylagh and Banagh, 1611. [Carew pp 630/65]

KERR, JAMES, a Scots-Irish student at Glasgow University in 1705. [MUG#182]

KERR, ROBERT, Earl of Ancrum, 1578-1654.
[PRONI#T1060/3/15]

KERR, THOMAS, was appointed a Captain of the Inniskilling
Regiment of Foot on 14 July 1697. [DAL.IV.187]

KIDD, JOHN, master of the Janet of McGee arrived in Ayr on 24
May 1673 from Ireland; master of the James of Portaferry
arrived in the Clyde in November 1695 from Dublin.
[NAS.E72.3.3; E72.19.23]

KILPATRICK, JOHN, a Scots-Irish student at Glasgow
University in 1699. [MUG#167]

KILPATRICK, HALBERT, merchant on the Katherine of
Londonderry at Port Glasgow in January 1691.
[NAS.E72.19.21]

KINKEDD, JOHN, in County Tyrone, 1636. [CSPIre.#CCLV]

KIRK, JOHN, master of the Dove of Dublin arrived in Glasgow on
24 May 1686 from Dublin. [NAS.E72.19.12]

KIRKWOOD, GEORGE, a Scots-Irish student at Glasgow
University in 1703. [MUG#179]

KIRKWOOD, JAMES, a Scots-Irish student at Glasgow
University in 1703. [MUG#179]

KIRKWOOD, JOHN, master of the Mary of Belfast arrrrived in
Glasgow on 2 March 1689 from Whitehaven.
[NAS.E72.19.14]

KNOUCLES, PETER, customs collector of Belfast, 1689.
[RPCS.XVI.310]

KNOX, ALEXANDER, a defender at the Siege of Derry, 29 July
1689. [WDSD]

KNOX, ANDREW, Bishop of the Isles of Scotland was elected as
Bishop of Raphoe, Ireland, in 1610. [CSPIre.Docquet Book]

KNOX, ANDREW, a Lieutenant of the Inniskilling Dragoons in 1689. [DAL.III.35]

KNOX, JAMES, Ensign of the Inniskilling Regiment of Foot, 1693. [DAL.III.336]

KNOX, JAMES, a Scots-Irish student at Glasgow University in 1699. [MUG#167]

KNOX, JOHN, in Rathfryland, northern Ireland, 1710. [NAS.CH1/2/30/386]

KNOX, THOMAS, a Scots-Irish student at Glasgow University in 1704. [MUG#180]

KNYLAND, HUGH, Strabane Muster Roll of 1630. [PRONI#T808/15164]

KYLE, JAMES, a burgess of Bangor, County Down, 25 November 1612. [CSPIre#Carte pp.62/117]

LAIRD, JOHN, master of the Swan of Donaghadee, 80 tons, from Ayr, Scotland, via Belfast, Ireland, to Virginia in 1689. [NAS.E72.3.20/21]

LAMONT, JOHN, master of the Blessing of Belfast arrived in Glasgow on 14 March 1667 from Carrickfergus. [NAS.E72.10.1]

LAUDER, ROBERT, Captain of the Earl of Dunbarton's Regiment at Kinsale in April 1679. [HMC.Ormonde.II.219]

LAURENCE, JOHN, in Killybegs, 1725. [NAS.GD10/944]

LAURIE, WILLIAM, a Scots-Irish student at Glasgow University in 1701. [MUG#172]

LEAGH, EDWARD, an Irishman who was captured in Kirkcudbright and imprisoned in Edinburgh Tolbooth during 1641. [RPCS.VII.210/221]

LEARD, FRANCIS, a Scots-Irish student at Glasgow University in 1699. [MUG#167]

LECKIE, ROBERT, a Scots-Irish student at Glasgow University in 1701. [MUG#171]

LECKY, ALEXANDER, 1631. [PRONI#T452]

LECKY, JOHN, in 1627 he became a founder burgess of St Johnstown, County Longford. [CPR#250]

LECKY, WALTER, was granted land in County Longford on 28 May 1625, by 1630 these lands had been exchanged for lands in County Leitrim; in 1627 he became a founder burgess of St Johnstown, County Longford. [CPR#55/567/250]

LEE, GEORGE, master of the Mary of Cork at the port of Inverness in September 1716. [NAS.E508.10.6]

LEEBIT, GEORGE, in Tullyhogue, County Tyrone, 1610. [Tullyhogue Muster Roll]

LEES, ANDREW, merchant on the Elizabeth of Portavadie arrived in the Clyde in April 1696 from Belfast. [NAS.E72.19.23]

LEIRMONTH, ADAM, son of Patrick Leirmonth, once in Aberlady then in Ireland, 1661. [RGS.XI.77]

LENNOX, ALEXANDER, master of the Isobel of Donaghadie at Port Patrick on 19 July 1682. [NAS.E72.20.7]

LENNOX, JOHN, was appointed vicar of Trevet, County Meath, on 18 January 1632. [CPR#594]

LENNOX, JOHN, master of the Iona of Donaghadie at Port Patrick on 27 July 1682. [NAS.E72.20.7]

LESLEY, HENRY, was appointed Dean of Down on 30 March 1627, then was appointed treasurer of the Cathedral of St Patrick, Dublin, on 21 July 1628; was granted several rectories and vicarages in County Down on 20 May 1631. [CPR#317/328/575]

LESLIE, ALEXANDER, 1st Earl of Leven, 1580-1661. [PRONI#T426]

LESLIE, JOHN, 1671. [PRONI#T415]

LESLIE, JOHN, eldest son of the Reverend Doctor John Leslie, the Rector of Urney, County Londonderry, a Captain of the Inniskilling Dragoons in 1689, killed at Aughrim. [DAL.III.35]

LESLIE, JOHN, master of the Recovery of Coleraine at Port Glasgow in January 1691. [NAS.E72.19.21]

LESLIE, JOSEPH, master of the Phoenix of Coleraine from the Clyde to Belfast on 18 February 1691. [NAS.E72.19.22]

LENNOX, ALEXANDER, master of the Isobel of Donaghadie arrived in Port Patrick on 15 November 1680 from Donaghadie. [NAS.E72.20.5]

LIDDELL, JOHN, a minister at Glenchie, Ireland, around 1712. [NAS.RS35.XII.356]

LIN, HENRY, a merchant at Templepark, Donegal, 14 July 1658. [NAS.R.S.Ayr#9/348]

LINDSAY, ANDREW, a Lieutenant of the Inniskilling Dragoons in 1689. [DAL.III.35]

LINDSAY, ANDREW, was appointed Lieutenant of Conygham's Regiment of Dragoons in 1694. [DAL.IV.15]

LINDSAY, BERNARD, with a sword, Tullyhogue, County Tyrone, 1610. [Tullyhogue Muster Roll]

LINDSAY, JOHN, 1686-1761. [PRONI#LPC1373]

LINDSAY, ROBERT, an undertaker with 1000 men in Tullyhogue, County Tyrone, 1610. [Muster Roll of Tullyhogue]

LINDSAY, ROBERT, a gentleman in County Longford, 1626. [CPR#151]

LINDSAY, ROBERT, a defender at the Siege of Derry, 29 July 1689. [WDSD]

LINDSAY, ROBERT, 1679-1742. [PRONI#D889/1/1B]

LINDSAY, THOMAS, 1724. [PRONI#T448/210/134]

LINDSAY, WILLIAM, soldier of Colonel Bayly's Company in February 1648. [HMC.Ormonde.II.70]

LISK, DAVID, petitioned the Scots Parliament for losses incurred by him in Ireland, 1641. [APS.V.appx.694]

LISK, ROBERT, son of the late Thomas Lisk in Balleneur in Ireland, was apprenticed to John Cook, a weaver in Edinburgh, on 23 April 1645. [REA]

LITTLE, THOMAS, master of the Watch of Donaghadie at Port Patrick on 10 May 1684. [NAS.E72.20.10]

LITTLE, THOMAS, a Scots-Irish student at Glasgow University in 1704. [MUG#180]

LIVINGSTONE, ALEXANDER, 1st Earl of Linlithgow, 1621. [PRONI#T2189]

LIVINGSTONE, ROBERT, Lieutenant of the Earl of Dunbarton's Regiment at Kinsale in April 1679. [HMC.Ormonde.II.219]

LIVINGSTONE, WILLIAM, a Scots-Irish student at Glasgow University in 1704. [MUG#180]

LOCKHART, GEORGE, merchant of the Recovery of Donaghadie arrived in the Clyde in October 1695 from Londonderry. [NAS.E72.19.23]

LOCKHART, LUCIUS, Captain of the Earl of Dunbarton's Regiment at Kinsale in April 1679. [HMC.Ormonde.II.219]

LOCKHART, RICHARD, Ensign of the Earl of Dunbarton's Regiment at Kinsale in April 1679. [HMC.Ormonde.II.219]

LOGAN, JOHN, a defender at the Siege of Derry, 29 July 1689. [WDSD]

LOGAN, ROBERT, in Broadyland, Ireland, heir to his uncle Walter Logan, there, 10 July 1669. [NAS.GD97.Sec.1/511]

LORIMER, JOHN, master of the Providence of Belfast arrived in Glasgow on 23 August 1686 from Belfast, [NAS.E72.119.12]; arrived at Port Glasgow in September 1689 from Montserrat. [NAS.E72.19.14]

LOSK, ALEXANDER, master of the Margaret of Holywood arrived in Glasgow on 31 October 1670 from Belfast. [NAS.E72.10.2]

LOUCKE, WILLIAM, a leaseholder of Ballyhebistocke, 5 February 1620, died 20 June 1623, father of Thomas. [MA#440]

LOVE, WILLIAM, master and merchant of the Elizabeth of Ayr arrived in Ayr on 17 February 1681 from Belfast. [NAS.E72.3.4]

LOWRY, HENRY, master of the Margaret of Strangford at Port Patrick on 30 August 1683. [NAS.E72.20.8]

LUKE, NINIAN, merchant on the Joan of Belfast from Port Glasgow to Madeira in May 1691. [NAS.E72.19.22]

LUNDIE, ROBERT, Captain of the Earl of Dunbarton's Regiment at Kinsale in April 1679. [HMC.Ormonde.II.219]; Governor of Londonderry in 1689. [NAS.GD26.7.37.1-3]

LYNG, RICHARD, an Irishman in Welshford, 1595. [Kirkcudbright Town Council Records, 2.5.1595]

LYNN, SAMUEL, a passenger on the Isabel of Magee Arrived in Ayr on 15 August 1673 from Ireland. [NAS.E72.3.3]

LYON, JOHN, master and merchant of the Elizabeth of Londonderry at Port Glasgow in March 1691. [NAS.E72.19.21]

MCADAM, DANIEL, master of the Salmond of Coleraine arrived in the Clyde in February 1696 from Coleraine.[NAS.E72.19.23]

MCALESTER, DONALD, from Ireland, in Kingarth in 1693. [Kingarth Kirk Session Records, 12.3.1693]

MCALEXANDER, THOMAS, a burgess of Bangor, County Down, 25 November 1612. [CSPIre#Carte pp.62/117]

MACALMOND, JOHN, a husbandman of Island Magee, County Antrim, see deposition dated 14 May 1652. [ISC.I.274]

MCAULAY, PATRICK, a Scots-Irish student at Glasgow University in 1699. [MUG#167]

MCBRIDE, DAVID, a Scots-Irish student at Glasgow University in 1702. [MUG#173]

MCBRIDE, ROBERT, a Scots-Irish student at Glasgow University in 1702. [MUG#174]

MCBROA, ROBERT, a passenger on the Margaret of Irvine which arrived in Ayr on 9 July 1673 from Strangford. [NAS.E72.3.3]

MCBRYDE, HENDRY, master of the Robert of Ballyshannon arrived in Port Glasgow in March 1691 from Killybegs. [NAS.E72.19.21]

MCCAFFIE, GEORGE, with a sword and snaphance, Tulluhogue, County Tyrone, 1610. [Tullyhogue Muster Roll]

MCCALL, JOHN, a Scots-Irish student at Glasgow University in 1702. [MUG#174]

MCCARTIE, DONOCHIE, son and heir of Lord Muskerde in Ireland, was admitted as a baronet of Nova Scotia on 29 April 1704. [NAS]

MCCARTIEMORE, FLORENS, a merchant in Donaghadie, was admitted as a burgess of Glasgow on 12 September 1707. [GBR]

MACCARTNEY, GEORGE, in Carrickfergus, 1658. [CSPIre#CCLXXXVII/96]

MACCARTNEY, GEORGE, the sovereign of Belfast, 1689.
[RPCS.XVI.310]

MACCARTNEY, ISAAC, in Belfast, 1728.
[NAS.NRAS#631/4/bundle A903]

MACCARTNEY, JAMES, a defender at the Siege of Derry, 29
July 1689. [WDSD]

MCCARTNEY, JAMES, a Scots-Irish student at Glasgow
University in 1699. [MUG#166]

MCCARTNEY, JOHN, master of the Lewis of Belfast arrived in
the Clyde in October 1695 from Belfast. [NAS.E72.19.23]

MCCLELLAND, JOHN, a defender at the Siege of Derry, 29 July
1689. [WDSD]

MCCLELLAND, JOHN, a Scots-Irish student at Glasgow
University in 1703. [MUG#177]

MCCLENAGHAN, JOHN, in Auchaley, Drumra parish, Omagh,
1666. [Hearth Money Roll]

MCCLENNANY, MATTHEW, a defender at the Siege of Derry,
29 July 1689. [WDSD]

MCCLEUCHAN, JOHN, a Scots-Irish student at Glasgow
University in 1703. [MUG#177]

MCCLINGAN, ALEXANDER, fled to Ireland between 1679 and
1689. [Penningham KSR, 19.2.1711]

MCCOLAN, THOMAS, master of the Merchant of Larne arrived
in the Clyde in December 1695 from Belfast.
[NAS.E72.19.23]

MCCOLMAN, JOHN OGE, a debtor in Ireland of Lord Antrim in
1638. [MA#476]

MCCONCHY, THOMAS, Scots-Irish student at Glasgow
University in 1702. [MUG#174]

SCOTS-IRISH LINKS

MCCONNELL, ARCHIBALD, master of the Margaret of Donaghadie at Port Patrick on 24 May 1672. [NAS.E72.20.3]

MCCONNELL, JAMES, master of the Marian of Larne from Irvine to Ireland on 14 April 1681; master of the Helen of Lochlarne arrived in the Clyde from Carrickfergus on 26 September 1691. [NAS.E72.12.3; E72.19.21]

MCCONNELL, JOHN, in Tullyhogue, County Tyrone, 1610. [Tullyhogue Muster Roll]

MCCONNELL, PHENNEL, wife of Matthew Hammel, with her six children, fled to Scotland by 1642. [SLT#150]

MCCONNELL, ..., son of James McConnell, leader of 4000 Scots, was granted lands in the Ards and Lecale on 25 April 1581. [CSPIre. LXXXII]

MCCONNOCHIE, ALLAN, in Ireland prior to 1664. [Kingarth Kirk Session Records, 25.4.1664]

MCCONNOCHIE, JAMES, master on the James of Belfast arrived in the Clyde on 5 November 1695 from Belfast. [NAS.E72.19.23]

MCCONNOCHY, ANDREW, master of the John of Larne arrived in Glasgow on 30 January 1689 from Belfast. [NAS.E72.1914]

MCCONNOCHY, DONALD, master of the Nonsuch of Coleraine arrived in Port Glasgow on 5 June 1683 from Coleraine. [NAS.E72.19.8]

MCCORMICK, JAMES, a defender at the Siege of Derry, 29 July 1689. [WDSD]; a Captain of the Londonderry Regiment of Foot in 1689. [DAL.III.83]

MCCORMICK, JOHN, master of the John of Portaferry arrived in the Clyde in June 1691 from Strangford. [NAS.E72.19.21]

MCCOSH, WILLIAM, master of the Jonas of Donaghadie at Port Patrick on 1 August 1672. [NAS.E72.20.4]

MCCRACKEN, JAMES, Lieutenant of the Earl of Dunbarton's Regiment at Kinsale in April 1679. [HMC.Ormonde.II.219]

MCCRAKAN, ALEXANDER, a Scots-Irish student at Glasgow University in 1702. [MUG#173]

MCCULLOCH, ROBERT, from Ireland, in Penningham in October 1705. [Penningham KSR, 31.10.1705]

MCCULLOUGH, ANTHONY, Lieutenant of a Londonderry or Inniskilling Regiment in 1690. [DAL.III.168]

MCCULLOUGH, HENRY, a Captain of the Londonderry Regiment of Foot in 1689. [DAL.III.83]

MCCULLOUGH, JAMES, of Island Magee, born around 1603, Captain of a company of foot soldier in Carrickfergus in 1641, see deposition dated 1 June 1653. [ISC.I.274]

MCCULLOUGH, JOHN, a Lieutenant of the Londonderry Regiment of Foot in 1689. [DAL.III.83]

MCCULLOUGH, WILLIAM, an Ensign of the Londonderry Regiment of Foot in 1689. [DAL.III.83]

MCDILSHENDER, ANDREW, in Tullyhogue, County Tyrone, 1610. [Tullyhogue Muster Roll]

MCDONALD, ALASDAIR MACCOLLA, from Ireland to Islay in 1640 with 70 men. [NAS.112.39..83..4-7; 83-84]

MCDONALD, Colonel DONALD, Dublin Castle, 1689. [NAS.RH4/90/5-6-7]

MCDONALD, JOHN, of Borncitaik, Captain of Colonel Donald McDonald's regiment, 1689. [NAS.RH4.90.7]

MCDONNELL, ANGUS, and his mother Lady Campbell, went from Ireland to the King's Court in Scotland in April 1585. [CalSPIre.CXVI]

MCDONNELL, DONNELL GORME, son of Lady Agnes Campbell, swore fealty for lands of Misset or Bisset in the Glinns, 18 September 1584. [CalSPIre.CXII]

MCDONNELL, EANEAS, 1675-1720. [PRONI#T1843]

MVDONNELL, JAMES, at Ould Stoul, 1642. [NAS.GD406.1.1308]

MCDONNELL, JAMES MACSORLEY, 1675-1720. [PRONI#T695/507]

MCDONNELL, ROSE, 1690. [PRONI#D262/128]

MCDONNELL, THOMAS, a Scots-Irish student at Glasgow University in 1701. [MUG#171]

MCDOUGALL, EUTHRED, a burgess of Strabane, County Tyrone, 25 November 1612. [CSPIre#Carte.pp62/117]

MCDOUGALL, JAMES, of Garthland, to Ireland in 1645. [NAS.PA7/3/102]

MCDOUGALL, PATRICK, a burgess of Strabane, County Tyrone, 25 November 1612. [CSPIre#Carte.pp62/117]

MCDOUALL, PATRICK, of Freuch, 1728. [NAS.NRAS#631/4/bundle A903]

MCDOWALL, MARIE, spouse of John McCulloch, in Ireland, 8 June 1642. [NAS.R.S.Ayr#7/448]

MCDOWELL, JAMES, a Scots-Irish student at Glasgow University in 1703. [MUG#177]

MCGEE, JEAN, was born about 1686, daughter of .... McGee and Mary Dickie, from Scotland to Ireland, settled in County Antrim by June 1698. [RGSU#31]

MCGEE, JOHN, master of the <u>Marion of Strangford</u> from Port Glasgow on 3 November 1680 to Belfast; master of the <u>John of Ballyshannon</u> arrived in the Clyde from Ballyshannon in March 1691. [NAS.E72.19.2/21]

MCGHIE, JOHN, from Ireland, in Penningham in May 1714. [Penningham KSR, 13.5.1714]

MCGIE, ANDREW, from Ireland, was admitted a burgess and guildsbrother of Ayr on 3 July 1676. [Ayr Burgess Roll]

MCGILL, ANNIE, a spinster in Red Bay, County Antrim, see deposition dated 9 April 1653. [ISC.I.258]

MCGILL, JAMES, a servant to William Pinkston a merchant in Donaghadie, was admitted as a burgess of Glasgow on 12 September 1707. [GBR]

MCGILL, JOHN, master of the Joan of Belfast from Port Glasgow on 21 January 1682 bound for Belfast; master of the London of Donaghadie, arrived in Glasgow on 9 May 1684 from Dublin. [NAS.E72.19.6/9]

MCGOUGH, JOHN, born 1618, residing in Carrickfergus, see deposition dated 27 may 1653. [ISC.I.264]

MACGOWAN, ALEXANDER, was appointed a Cornet of the Regiment of Irish Dragoons on 1 July 1699. [DAL.IV.221]

MCGRIFFIN, ROBERT, in Tullyhogue, County Tyrone, 1610. [Tullyhogue Muster Roll]

MCGUFFOCK, JOHN, in Ireland, 1711. [Penninghame Kirk Session Records, 8.11.1711]

MCGUFFOG, HUGH, a Scots-Irish student at Glasgow University in 1704. [MUG#180]

MCHAFFIE, JOHN, master of the Archibald of Donaghadie at Port Patrick on 25 September 1684. [NAS.E72.20.9]

MCHAFFIE, JOHN, from Ireland, in Penningham in November 1707. [Penningham KSR, 11.11.1707]

MCHARG, JOHN, with his wife and three children, from Ireland to Dumfries in 1690. [NAS.CH2.537.15.1/36]

MCILVRINI, GILMORIE, and his son Archibald, from Ireland, in Rothesay in July 1670. [Rothesay Town Council Records, 12.7.1670]

MCILWAIN, ANDREW, Lieutenant of the Inniskilling Regiment of Foot in 1691. [DAL.III.206]

MCILWAYNE, NEIL, provost, Strabane Muster Roll of 1630. [PRONI#T808/15164]

MCINTURNER, DUNCAN, in Turlane, Drumra parish, Omagh, 1666. [Hearth Money Roll]

MCKAIG, JOHN, from Ireland to Dumfries in 1690. [NAS.CH2.537.15.1/35]

MCKAY, DANIEL, was granted lands of Ballyterim, Loughans, and Farrenmecallin, died 20 May 1622, father of Alexander or Alaster. [NA#440]

MCKAY, DONALD, a landowner in the parish of Maghrasharkan, barony of Killenway, 1660. [MA#466]

MCKAY, ROBERT, was appointed Major of Colonel Erle's Regiment on 1 August 1691. [DAL.III.217]

MCKEAN, DANIEL, an Irish student at Glasgow University in 1700. [MUG#169]

MCKEDYON, ANDREW, in Tullyhogue, County Tyrone, 1610. [Tullyhogue Muster Roll]

MCKEILLOR, DUNCAN, a rebel who was transported from Belfast to Galloway in 1685. [RPCS.XI.165]

MCKENNA, WILLIAM, a merchant in Belfast, petitioned the General Assembly of the Church of Scotland on 5 August 1643. [AGA#74]

MCKENNY, ALEXANDER, a burgess of Rathmullen, County Donegal, 18 November 1612. [CSPIre.Carte pp62/87]

MCKENNY, RORY, chaplain to the Earl of Dunbarton's Regiment at Kinsale in April 1679. [HMC.Ormonde.II.220]

MCKENZIE, MURDO, Lieutenant of the Earl of Dunbarton's Regiment at Kinsale in April 1679. [HMC.Ormonde.II.219]

MCKERLIE, WILLIAM, in Downpatrick, was admitted as a burgess and freeman of Rothesay on 6 December 1665. [Rothesay Town Council Records, 6.12.1665]

MACKHEN, Captain, master of the William of Portaferry, which was seized off Virginia in 1697. [SPAWI.1697/1130]

MCKIMMIE, ALEXANDER, master of the Anna of Belfast arrived in the Clyde from Dublin in January 1696. [NAS.E72.19.23]

MCKINLAY, DANIEL, master of the Robert of Belfast arrived in Glasgow on 4 October 1686 from Belfast. [NAS.E72.19.12]

MCKINLAY, ROBERT, master and merchant of the Providence of Belfast from Irvine to Belfast on 4 July 1682. [NAS.E72.12.6]

MACKINTOSH, MALCOLM, Ensign of the Earl of Dunbarton's Regiment at Kinsale in April 1679. [HMC.Ormonde.II.219]

MCKITRICK, ANDREW, a Scots-Irish student at Glasgow University in 1702. [MUG#173]

MCKITRICK, JOHN, master and merchant of the John of Portaferry from Irvine to Ireland on 25 April 1681. [NAS.E72.12.3]

MCKNEIGHT, WILLIAM, an Irish student at Glasgow University in 1702. [MUG#174]

MCLACHLANE, JOHN, a Scots-Irish student at Glasgow University in 1703. [MUG#178]

MCLAGHLIN, GEORGE, a landowner in Ardmoy parish, and in the parish of Billy, barony of Carey 1660. [MA#466]

MCLANE, JOHN, was appointed chaplain to the Regiment of Irish Dragoons on 1 December 1699. [DAL.IV.221]

MCLEOD, HENRY, [Henry McLoade], leader of 2000 Scots, was granted lands in the Ards and Lecale on 25 April 1581. [Cal.SPIre.LXXXII]

MCLEOD, LEWIS, [Loyes McLoade], leader of 2000 Scots, was granted lands in the Ards and Lecale on 25 April 1581. [Cal.SPIre.LXXXII]

MCMACHEN, JOHN, master of the Janet of Belfast at the port of Ayr in November 1714, [NAS.E508.8.6]

MCMAINS, JOHN, a Scots-Irish student at Glasgow University in 1701. [MUG#171]

MCMEIHAN, THOMAS, a Scots-Irish student at Glasgow University in 1702. [MUG#174]

MCMILLAN, JAMES, a Scots-Irish student at Glasgow University in 1702. [MUG#174]

MCMIN, THOMAS, from Ireland to Dumfries in 1690. [NAS.CH2.537.15.1/35]

MCMULLOCH, ARCHIBALD, a defender at the Siege of Derry, 29 July 1689. [WDSD]

MCMURRAY, DAVID, a Scots-Irish student at Glasgow University in 1704. [MUG#180]

MCMURRAY, THOMAS, master of the John of Portaferry arrived in the Clyde in June 1691 from Strangford. [NAS.E72.19.21]

MCMURTAN, ROBERT, with a sword and callance, Tullyhogue, County Tyrone, 1610. [Muster Roll of Tullyhogue]

MCNAMIE, PATRICK, servant of Gordon O'Neill in Londonderry, was admitted a burgess and guildsbrother of Ayr on 3 July 1676. [Ayr Burgess Roll]

MCNAUGHTON, DONNELL, son and heir of John McNaughton who died on 10 March 1630, agent for the Antrim estates and a leaseholder in the barony of Dunluce in 1637, father of John. [MA#438]

MCNAUGHTON, JOHN, from Scotland to Ireland, settled as a leaseholder of Ballymagarry near Dunluce Castle, died 10 March 1630. [MA#439]

MCNAUGHTON, Mrs, a widow and a debtor in Ireland of Lord Antrim in 1638. [MA#476]

MCNEALL, JOHN, a Scots-Irish student at Glasgow University in 1704. [MUG#181]

MCNEE, ROBERT, an Irish student at Glasgow University in 1705. [MUG#182]

MCNEILL, HECTOR, master of the Speedwell of Lochlarne arrived in Glasgow on 2 August 1686 from Dublin. [NAS.E72.19.12]

MCPHEADRIS, JOHN, an Irish student at Glasgow University in 1700. [MUG#169]

MCPHERSON, JOHN, fled to Ireland, father of Jane Stewart's child in Kingarth, Bute, 1693. [Kingarth Kirk Session Records, 12.10.1693]

MCQUILLING, RORY OG, of Glenachartie, County Antrim, gentleman, and his wife Mary Necttenyse O'Neil, leased lands of Tuisder from Archibald Edmonstone of Braidyland, dated at Ballimenacht, 8 May 1628. [NAS.GD97.Sec.1/390]

MCTAGGART, MICHAEL, with his family, fled to Ireland between 1679 and 1689. [Penningham KSR, 19.2.1711]

MCVARICH, PATRICK, in Ireland, 1720. [NAS.Argyll Sheriff Court Book #VII, 29.12.1720]

MCWILLIAM, JOHN, master of the Janet of Belfast, from Scotland to Ostend, Flanders, in 1716/1717. [NAS.E508]

MAINE, JOHN, master of the Salmon of Belfast arrived in Port Glasgow on 4 November 1695. [NAS.E72.19.23]

MANSON, JAMES, a defender at the Siege of Derry, 29 July 1689. [WDSD]

MANSON, THEOPHILIS, a defender at the Siege of Derry, 29 July 1689. [WDSD]

MANSON, WILLIAM, a defender at the Siege of Derry, 29 July 1689. [WDSD]

MARSHALL, WILLIAM, merchant of the Elizabeth of Belfast arrived in the Clyde from Belfast in November 1695; and of the Anthony of Glenarme arrived in the Clyde in February 1696 from Belfast. [NAS.E72.19.23; E72.19.23]

MARTIN, ANTONY, 1650. [PRONI#T1075/6/67]

MARTIN, Mrs DOROTHY, a widow, sometime in Dublin, then in Edinburgh, 1728. [ECA.Moses.159/6067]

MARTIN, JAMES, fled to Ireland between 1679 and 1689. [Penningham KSR, 19.2.1711]

MARTIN, JAMES, a Scots-Irish student at Glasgow University in 1702. [MUG#174]

MARTIN, JOHN, master of the Jean of Donaghadie arrived in Glasgow in January 1666 from Belfast. [NAS.E72.10.1]

MARTIN, JOHN, in Glenvogie, fled to Ireland between 1679 and 1689. [Penningham KSR, 19.2.1711]

MARTIN, JOHN, a minister in Ireland, husband of Helen, daughter of James Fairie a hammerman, was admitted as a burgess and guilds-brother of Glasgow on 2 July 1708. [GBR]

MARTIN, ROBERT, master of the Agnes of Belfast arrived in Glasgow on 1 January 1673 from Belfast. [NAS.E72.10.3]

MARTIN, ROBERT, a merchant in Belfast, 1689. [RPCS.XVI.310]

MARTIN, ROBERT, from Ireland to Dumfries in 1690.
[NAS.CH2.537.15.1/25]

MATHER, ROBERT, master of the Three ..... of Belfast at Port
Patrick on 20 October 1682. [NAS.E72.20.7]

MAULE, THOMAS, born in Dublin, brown hair, trooper of the
King's Guard of Horse from 1672, later in Ireland.
[HMC.Ormonde.II.238]

MAXWELL, AGNES, daughter of the late Robert Maxwell the
younger a maltman in County Tyrone, 1650. [RGS.X.502]

MAXWELL, ALEXANDER, from Halls, Tynwald, to Ireland by
1690. [NAS.CH2.537.15.2/75-98]

MAXWELL, Sir GEORGE, 1720. [PRONI#T640]

MAXWELL, HENRY, 1640-1709. [PRONI#T848/28]

MAXWELL, HENRY, 1650. [PRONI#T640]

MAXWELL, HENRY, 1670. [PRONI#T1007/9]

MAXWELL, HERBERT, in Lecale, County Down, 19 September
1614. [CSPIre.Docquet Book]

MAXWELL, JAMES, Ensign of the Earl of Dunbarton's Regiment
at Kinsale in April 1679. [HMC.Ormonde.II.219]

MAXWELL, JAMES, in Pettigo, Ireland, 1715.
[NAS.RD4.117.876]

MAXWELL, Sir JOHN, granted a commission on 3 March 1630.
[CPR#572]

MAXWELL, JOHN, in Strabane, 1697. [Kingarth Kirk Session
Records, 22.11.1697]

MAXWELL, JOHN, 1706. [PRONI#D363]

MAXWELL, ROBERT, a minister, 1609; was appointed Archdeacon of Down on 18 August 1628. [CPR#328]

MAXWELL, Sir ROBERT, 1595-1672. [PRONI#T729/2]

MAXWELL, ROBERT, son in law of Lord Kirkcudbright, in Londonderry, 1630s. [NAS.RH15.91/9, 46]

MAXWELL, Dr ROBERT, rector of Tinane, County Armagh, see deposition dated 22 August 1642. [ISC.I.326]

MAXWELL, WILLIAM, in Tullyhogue, County Tyrone, 1610. [Tullyhogue Muster Roll]

MAXWELL, WILLIAM, merchant on the Elizabeth of Londonderry at Port Glasgow on 27 January 1691. [NAS.E72.19.21]

MAXWELL, WILLIAM, from Ireland, in Penningham in May 1714. [Penningham KSR, 13.5.1714]

MELDRUM, Captain JOHN, recommended by King Janes for service in Ireland on 17 April 1611. [CSPIre.]

MELVILLE, PATRICK, Captain of the Earl of Dunbarton's Regiment at Kinsale in April 1679. [HMC.Ormonde.II.219]

MIDDLETON, GEORGE, an apothecary, in Kilkenny 1689, son of Major Robert Middleton in Leith. [NAS.GD406.1.3510]

MILDMAY, DANIEL, in Lisburne, 1689. [RPCS.XIV.502]

MILDMAY, RICHARD, from Lisburne, died in Ayr during April 1689. [RPCS.XIV.502]

MILLER, HEW, master of the Janet of Glenarme arrived in Glasgow in May 1667 from Carrickfergus. [NAS.E72.10.1]

MILLET, WILLIAM, an Irish student at Glasgow University in 1705. [MUG#183]

MILLIKEN, THOMAS, a merchant in Balliwalter, was admitted as a burgess and guilds-brother of Ayr by right of his wife

Jean, daughter of the late John Muir, a merchant, burgess and guilds-brother of Ayr, on 4 April 1665. [Ayr Burgess Roll]

MILLING, JAMES, master of the Margaret of Donaghadie at Port Patrick on 19 August 1681. [NAS.E72.20.5]

MILLING, JOHN, master of the Blessing of Donaghadee from Whitehaven to Port Glasgow in December 1690. [NAS.E72.19.16]

MILLING, ROBERT, a Scots-Irish student at Glasgow University in 1698. [MUG#165]

MIRKE, JAMES, a minister in Ireland from around 1634 to 1641, fled to Scotland in 1642. [SLT#133]

MITCHELBURN, JOHN, in Londonderry, 1689. [NAS.GD406.1.3527]; son of Abraham Mitchelburn, a Captain of the Londonderry Regiment of Foot in 1689, fought at the Boyne and at the Siege of Sligo in 1691, died in Londonderry on 1 October 1721, buried in Glendermot churchyard. [DAL.III.83]

MITCHELHILL, JOHN, minister at Balliphilip, Ireland, son of John Mitchelhill a merchant burgess of Edinburgh, and his wife Barbara Gilchrist, a disposition dated 11 August 1625. [ECA.Moses.4/152]

MITCHELL, GEORGE, servant of Andrew **McGie,** from Ireland, was admitted a burgess and guildsbrother of Ayr on 3 July 1676. [Ayr Burgess Roll]

MITCHELL, JAMES, of Island Magee, see deposition of 1 June 1653. [ISC.I.256]

MITCHELL, JAMES, born in County Antrim, brown hair, trooper of the King's Guard of Horse from 1676, later in Ireland. [HMC.Ormonde.II.238]

MONCREIFF, DAVID, a burgess of Bangor, County Down, 25 November 1612. [CSPIre#Carte pp.62/117]

MONCREIFF, JAMES, Captain of the Earl of Dunbarton's Regiment at Kinsale in April 1679. [HMC.Ormonde.II.219]

MONFOD, HEW, master of the John of Glenarme arrived in Glasgow on 24 July 1666 from Coleraine. [NAS.E72.10.1]

MONROE, JOHN, chaplain to Mountjoy's Regiment of Foot in 1701. [DAL.IV.259]

MONTFORD, JOHN, master of the Janet of Larne arrived in Glasgow on 17 May 1672 from Carrickfergus. [NAS.E72.10.3]

MONTGOMERY, ADAM, of Braidstone, an alleged pirate from Ayr, was accused of attacking and robbing Thomas Copran, a merchant from Dublin, in northern Ireland during 1584. [RPCS.IV.1586]

MONTGOMERY, ALEXANDER, son of John Montgomery of Croghan, a Captain of the Inniskilling Dragoons in 1689, promoted to Lieutenant Colonel by 1706, possibly died in 1722. [DAL.III.35]

MONTGOMERY, ARCHIBALD, a constable of Donaghadee in 1647. [CSPIre#CCLXIII]

MONTGOMERY, Mrs DENNEY, widow of James Montgomery a cleric, parson of Donnamayne, County Monaghan, see deposition dated 17 November 1642. [ISC.II.27]

MONTGOMERY, FRANCIS, a Scots-Irish student at Glasgow University in 1702. [MUG#174]

MONTGOMERY, GEORGE, 1621. [PRONI#T1075/8/30]

MONTGOMERY, GEORGE, quartermaster to the Ulster Horse at Donaghadie in July 1680. [HMC.Ormonde.II.227]

MONTGOMERY, GILBERT, a burgess of Clogher, 12 December 1612. [CSPIre.Carte pp62/77]

MONTGOMERY, HAMILTON, Ensign of Mountjoy's Regiment of Foot, 1694, appointed a Lieutenant in the regiment on 20 January 1697. [DAL.III.391; IV.191/259]

MONTGOMERY, HUGH, 1560-1630. [PRONI#T640, etc]

MONTGOMERY, HUGH, a burgess of Clogher, 12 December 1612. [CSPIre.Carte pp62/77]

MONTGOMERY, HUGH, 1st Earl of Mount Alexander, 1625-1663. [PRONI#D562/1]

MONTGOMERY, HUGH, 2na Earl of Mount Alexander, 1651-1717. [PRONI#T780/54]

MONTGOMERY, HUGH, in Omagh, 1666. [Hearth Money Roll]

MONTGOMERY, HUGH, a merchant in Belfast or Balliskeoch, was admitted as a burgess and guilds-brother of Ayr on 11 July 1687. [Ayr Burgess Roll]

MONTGOMERY, HUGH, possibly a Captain of the Inniskilling Regiment of Horse in 1689. [DAL.III.27]

MONTGOMERY, ISOBEL, in Ireland, petitioned the Scots Parliament, 1639. [APS.V.268]

MONTGOMERY, JAMES, a burgess of Killileagh, 17 November 1612. [CSPIre#Carte pp62/110]

MONTGOMERY, JAMES, a burgess of Bangor, County Down, 25 November 1612. [CSPIre#Carte pp.62/117]

MONTGOMERY, JAMES, a burgess of Clogher, 12 December 1612. [CSPIre.Carte pp62/77]

MONTGOMERY, JAMES, of Rouskie, County Fermanagh, granted land in County Fermanagh to Malcolm Hamilton, Lord Archbishop of Cashel on 10 May 1626. [CPR#609]

MONTGOMERY, JAMES, second son of Robert Montgomery, in County Fermanagh, 13 August 1623. [CPR#609]

MONTGOMERY, JAMES, 1630-1646. [PRONI#D627/1/2, etc]

MONTGOMERY, Colonel Sir JAMES, in Antrim 1645, in Belfast, 1647. [CSPIre.#CCLX; CCLXIII]

MONTGOMERY, JAMES, of Rosemount, County Down, 23 October 1696. [NAS.GD97.576]

MONTGOMERY, JOHN, a burgess of Clogher, 12 December 1612. [CSPIre.Carte pp62/77]

MONTGOMERY, JOHN, pardoned for the murder of James Hogg on 18 July 1628, but sentence to be burnt on the hand. [CPR#329]

MONTGOMERY, JOHN, eldest son of John Montgomery of Croghan, a Captain of the Inniskilling Dragoons in 1689, promoted to Major on 30 April 1696. [DAL.III.35; IV.120]

MONTGOMERY, KATHERINE, from Ireland to Dumfries in 1690. [NAS.CH2.537.15.1/27]

MONTGOMERY, NATHANIEL, master and merchant of the Relief of Glenarm from Irvine to Ireland on 17 February 1681. [NAS.E72.12.3]

MONTGOMERY, ROBERT, Provost of Clogher, 12 December 1612. [CSPIre.Carte pp62/77]

MONTGOMERY, ROBERT, a burgess of Newton Ards, County Down, 17 January 1612. [CSPIre.Carte pp62/84]

MONTGOMERY, ROBERT, the elder of Hazlehead, Scotland, was granted lands in County Fermanagh on 19 August 1618, which were granted to Robert Montgomery the younger of Rouskie on 6 August 1623. [CPR#609]

MONTGOMERY, ROBERT, the younger of Rouskie, was granted lands in County Fermanagh on 6 August 1623. [CPR#609]

MONTGOMERY, ROBERT, a Cornet of the Inniskilling Dragoons in 1695. [DAL.IV.61]

MONTGOMERIE, ROBERT, master of the <u>Anthony of Glenarme</u> arrived in the Clyde in February 1696 from Belfast. [NAS.E72.19.23]

MONTGOMERY, THOMAS, Provost of Newton Ards, County Down, 17 January 1612. [CSPIre.Carte pp62/84]

MONTGOMERY, THOMAS, master of the <u>John of Belfast</u> arrived in Glasgow on 29 August 1672 from Belfast. [NAS.E72.10.3]

MONTGOMERY, Sir THOMAS, in Ireland, probate 10 April 1716 PCC. [PRO.Prob.11/551]

MONTGOMERY, WILLIAM, a defender at the Siege of Derry, 29 July 1689. [WDSD]

MONTGOMERY, WILLIAM, master of the <u>Marie of Glenarme</u> from Irvine to Ireland on 15 June 1681; arrived in Port Glasgow on 24 May 1683 from Glenarme. [NAS.E72.12.3; E72.19.8]

MONTGOMERY, WILLIAM, a merchant in Dublin, was admitted as a burgess and guilds-brother of Ayr on 15 July 1717. [Ayr Burgess Roll]

MONYPENNY, ANDREW, clerk, Archdeacon of Connor, 1629. [NAS.GD97.Sec.1/398]

MONYPENNY, GEORGE, born in County Down, brown hair, trooper of the King's Guard of Horse from 1675, later in Ireland. [HMC.Ormonde.II.238]

MOOR, CHARLES, a Scots-Irish student at Glasgow University in 1702. [MUG#174]

MOOR, JAMES, a Scots-Irish student at Glasgow University in 1703. [MUG#177]

MOOR, JOHN, master of the <u>John of Glenarme</u> arrived in Ayr on 2 August 1673 from Ireland. [NAS,E72.3.3]

MOORE, Mrs JANE, wife of William Moore of Ballybregagh, received letters patent of denization on 5 July 1631. [CPR#59]

MORISON, CLEMENT, from Ireland, in Penningham in November 1706. [Penningham KSR, 27.11.1706]

MORNAY, HEW, master of the Jean and Catherine of Dublin arrived in Port Glasgow on 5 March 1690 from Dublin.[NAS.E72.19.18]

MOWAT, JOHN, Ensign of the Earl of Dunbarton's Regiment at Kinsale in April 1679. [HMC.Ormonde.II.219]

MUIR, ALEXANDER, a merchant in Belfast, who was admitted as a burgess and guilds-brother of Glasgow on 27 March 1674, a nephew of John Craig a merchant. [GBR]

MUIR, ANDREW, master of the Mayflower of Donaghadie at Port Patrick on 4 August 1683. [NAS.E72.20.8]

MUIR, CHARLES, son of John Muir a merchant in Dublin, was admitted as a burgess and guilds-brother of Glasgow on 6 August 1717. [GBR]

MUIR, JOHN, son of the late Andrew Muir in Belfast, County Antrim, was apprenticed to Gilbert Muir a merchant in Edinburgh on 15 January 1640, [REA]

MUIR, WILLIAM, son of James Muir in Caldrum, Ireland, was apprenticed to John Hamilton, a merchant in Edinburgh, on 18 November 1674. [REA]

MUIRHEAD, WILLIAM, a saddler in Antrim, husband of Isobel Lang, 13 September 1676. [NAS.GD97.Sec.1/540]

MUNRO, ALEXANDER, Lieutenant Colonel of the Earl of Dunbarton's Regiment at Kinsale in April 1679. [HMC.Ormonde.II.219]

MUNRO, ANDREW, Captain of the Earl of Dunbarton's Regiment at Kinsale in April 1679. [HMC.Ormonde.II.219]

MUNRO, HENRY, a defender at the Siege of Derry, 29 July 1689. [WDSD]

MUNRO, SUSANNAH, widow of John Munro of Welsetoun, County West Meath, and wife of Charles Stewart, 1715. [NAS.RD4.116.779]

MURDOCH, ARCHIBALD, a merchant in County Down, 1715. [NAS.RD3.146.120]

MURDOCH, JAMES, soldier of Colonel Bayly's Company in February 1648. [HMC.Ormonde.II.70]

MURDOCH, ROBERT, soldier of Colonel Bayly's Company in February 1648. [HMC.Ormonde.II.69]

MURDOCH, ROBERT, master of the Marian of Larne from Irvine to Ireland on 14 April 1681. [NAS.E72.12.3]

MURE, GAVIN, a Scots-Irish student at Glasgow University in 1701. [MUG#171]

MURRAY, ADAM, Colonel of a Londonderry or Inniskilling Regiment in 1690. [DAL.III.168]

MURRAY, ALEXANDER, son of James Murray of Sclonarie, at Ballichering, Ireland, 1620. [NAS.Argyll Sasines#1/137]

MURRAY, ARCHIBALD, Ensign of the Earl of Dunbarton's Regiment at Kinsale in April 1679. [HMC.Ormonde.II.219]

MURRAY, CHARLES, Adjutant of the Earl of Dunbarton's Regiment at Kinsale in April 1679. [HMC.Ormonde.II.220]

MURRAY, DANIEL, master of the James and Robert of Belfast, arrived in the Clyde in March 1696 from Belfast. [NAS.E72.19.23]

MURRAY, GEORGE, a Scots-Irish student at Glasgow University in 1702. [MUG#173]

MURRAY, JAMES, of Sclonarie, at Ballichering, Ireland, 1620. [NAS.Argyll Sasines#1/137]

MURRAY, JAMES, Captain of the Earl of Dunbarton's Regiment at Kinsale in April 1679. [HMC.Ormonde.II.219]

MURRAY, JAMES, a merchant in Sligo, was admitted as a burgess of Montrose in 1711. [Montrose Burgess Register]

MURRAY, JOHN, Captain of Mountjoy's Regiment of Foot, 1694. [DAL.III.391]

MURRAY, MATTHEW, in Ireland, 1692. [NAS.CH2.1284.2/147]

MURRAY, Sir PATRICK, a gentleman of HM Privy Chamber, and wife Elizabeth, to Ireland in 1612. [CSPIre]

MURRAY, PATRICK, was appointed Lieutenant of Mitchelburne's Regiment of Foot on 8 June 1694. [DAL.IV.41]

MURRAY, ROBERT, master of the George of Belfast from Port Glasgow to Belfast in September 1689. [NAS.E72.19.15]

MURRAY, ROBERT, master of the Jane of Belfast, from Belfast to Virginia in 1692 but captured by the French off Newfoundland on the return voyage. [PRO.HCA.Exams.Vol.80]; master of the Loyalty of Belfast, a 60 ton pink, to Virginia in 1699. [PRO.CO5/1441]

MURRAY, SAMUEL, Captain of a Londonderry or Inniskilling Regiment in 1690. [DAL.III.168]

MURRAY, ..., from Ireland, in Penningham in May 1703. [Penningham KSR, 7.5.1703]

MURRAY, Major, a Scots-Irish student at Glasgow University in 1704. [MUG#180]

MURROW, GEORGE, Lieutenant of the Earl of Dunbarton's Regiment at Kinsale in April 1679. [HMC.Ormonde.II.219]

MURROW, ROBERT, Lieutenant of the Earl of Dunbarton's Regiment at Kinsale in April 1679. [HMC.Ormonde.II.219]

MURTHLAND, ROBERT, master and merchant of the Relief of Glenarme at the port of Irvine on 6 December 1668; master and merchant on the Janet of Glenarme at the port of Irvine on 2 June 1669 [NAS.E72.12.1]

MURTLAND, ROBERT, merchant aboard the James of Carrickfergus which arrived in Ayr on 25 June 1673 from Ireland. [NAS.E72.3.3]

NAPIER, ROBERT, Lieutenant of a Regiment of Foot in Londonderry in July 1680. [HMC.Ormonde.II.226]

NCKAW, ISABEL, fled from Kingarth to Ireland 'being with child' in 1682. [Kingarth Kirk Session Records, 5.2.1682]

NEAVEN, JANET, parish of Billy, see deposition dated 9 March 1652. [ISC.I.244]

NEILIE, SAMUEL, from Ireland to Dumfries in 1690. [NAS.CH2.537.15.1/30]

NEILSON, GEORGE, a merchant in Ireland, 1665. [D BR Burgh Court Processes]

NEILSON, JOHN, in County Antrim, 1706. [NAS.NRAS#2522/CA3/7]

NEILSON, WILLIAM, from Ireland, in Penningham, 1709. [Penningham KSR, 4.5.1709]

NESBITT, ALBERT, son of Captain Andrew Nesbitt, a Lieutenant of the Inniskilling Dragoons in 1689. [DAL.III.35]

NESBITT, ANDREW, of Brenter, County Donegal, a Captain of the Inniskilling Dragoons in 1689, possibly died in 1692. [DAL.III.35]

NESBITT, ANDREW, was appointed Cornet of Conygham's Regiment of Dragoons in 1694. [DAL.IV.15]

NESBITT, JAMES, a cornet of the Inniskilling Dragoons in 1689. [DAL.III.35]

NESBITT, ROBERT, his wife **Emmeline,** and five children, John, Helen, Mary, Robert, and an infant, in Ardnaglass, barony of Tiroragh, County Sligo, all murdered by rebels in May 1643 with the exception of son Robert. See deposition 16 June 1653. [ISC.II.9]

NEVIN, THOMAS, a Scots-Irish student at Glasgow University in 1703. [MUG#177]

NEWBURGH. Mr, 1711. [NAS.GD406.1.5689]

NICOLSON, WILLIAM, 1655-1727. [PRONI#MIC69, etc]

NISBET, ALEXANDER, Dublin, 1727. [ECA.Moses.VI/158/6028]

NISBET, JAMES, son of the late Murdoch Nisbet in Lottrie in Ireland, was apprenticed to Thomas Adam, a tanner and marriken maker in Edinburgh, on 11 July 1655, [ERA]

NISBET, WILLIAM, a Cornet of the Irish Dragoons in 1693. [DAL.III.300]

NIXON, ROBERT, with a sword and snaphance, Tullyhogue, County Tyrone, 1610. [Muster Roll of Tullyhogue]

NIXON, ROBERT, in Tullyhogue, County Tyrone, 1610. [Tullyhogue Muster Roll]

NOBLE, ARTHUR, a defender at the Siege of Derry, 29 July 1689. [WDSD]

O'CONA, DENIS, a seaman from Waterford, a prisoner in Greenock, to be exchanged for a Scot in Irish hands, 1642. [RPCS.VII.339]

OGILVIE, JEREMY, in Carrickfergus, 1649. [GA#278]

OGILVY, JOHN, Master of the Revels in Ireland, 1649. [CSPIre#CCLXXVI/62]

OLIPHANT, Mrs CHRISTIAN, widow of William Oliphant a cleric, see deposition dated 3 February 1645. [ISC.I.363]

OLIPHANT, Reverend WILLIAM, was murdered by rebels in County Sligo in 1641. [ISC.I.363/365/367/368/370]

OLIVER, GEORGE, in Tullyhogue, County Tyrone, 1610. [Tullyhogue Muster Roll]

O'NEILL, GORDON, in Londonderry, was admitted as a burgess and guilds-brother of Ayr on 3 July 1676. [Ayr Burgess Roll]

ORR, EDWARD, master and merchant of the Janet of Glenarm arrived in Irvine on 11 December 1668 from Glenarme. [NAS.E72.12.1]

ORR, JAMES, a Scots-Irish student at Glasgow University in 1702. [MUG#174]

ORR, JEAN, with her children, to Ireland in 1701. [Kingarth Kirk Session Records, 11 May 1701]

ORR, JOHN, master of the Good Fortune of Coleraine, arrived in Glasgow on 14 December 1682 from Coleraine. [NAS.E72.19.8]

ORR, ROBERT, a Scots-Irish student at Glasgow University in 1703. [MUG#177]

ORR, WILLIAM, master of the Ann of Donaghadie arrived in Ayr on 14 February 1667 from Belfast. [NAS.E72.3.1]

ORR, WILLIAM, master of the Good Fortune of Coleraine arrived in Port Glasgow on 14 December 1682 from Coleraine. [NAS.E72.19.8]

ORUM, LAURENCE, an Irish merchant who arrived in Ayr in September 1672 on board the Unity of Ayr from Barbados, [AA.B6.18.4]

PATERSON, ADAM, servant to William Montgomery a merchant in Dublin, was admitted as a burgess and guilds-brother of Ayr on 15 July 1717. [Ayr Burgess Roll]

PATERSON, GEORGE, Strabane Muster Roll of 1630.
[PRONI#T808/15164]

PATERSON, ROBERT, son of the late Robert Paterson a merchant
in Dublin, was apprenticed to John Hewat, a cordiner, in
Edinburgh on 24 January 1649, transferred to John Duguid on
21 November 1649. [REA]

PATERSON, SUSANNA, from Ireland to Dumfries in 1690.
[NAS.CH2.537.15.1/30]

PATTEN, ARCHIBALD, Captain of the Earl of Donegal's
Regiment of Foot in 1701. [DAL.IV.257]

PATTERSON, ROBERT, in Newton, County Tyrone, 1636.
[CSPIre.#CCLV]

PATTERSON, SAMUEL, a Scots-Irish student at Glasgow
University in 1703. [MUG#178]

PATTERSON, THOMAS, from Ireland to Dumfries in 1690.
[NAS.CH2.537.15.1/28, 96]

PEAR, JOHN, in County Antrim, 1706.
[NAS.NRAS#2522/CA3/7]

PEARSON, ANDREW, in Tullyhogue, County Tyrone, 1610.
[Tullyhogue Muster Roll]

PEEBLES, ROBERT, in County Antrim, 1706.
[NAS.NRAS#2522/CA3/7]

PENROSE, JAMES, a merchant from Clonish, Ireland, who was
captured by the Turks when returning from Malaga, Spain, in
1685. [RPCS.XII.308]

PENROSE, RICHARD, a merchant in Clonish, Ireland, husband of
Margaret, 1685. [RPCS.XII.308]

PEOPLES, HUGH, a leaseholder in Ballyhebistocke, 19 October
1631. [MA#440]

PERRY, JOHN, in Camy, parish of Drumra, Omagh, 1666. [Hearth Money Roll]

PETER, THOMAS, merchant of the Alexander of Dublin, from the Clyde in December 1690 to Dublin; merchant of the Swallow of Carrickfergus which arrived in the Clyde in April 1691 from Dublin. [NAS.E72.19.21]

PIERSON, ALEXANDER, Lieutenant of the Earl of Dunbarton's Regiment at Kinsale in April 1679. [HMC.Ormonde.II.219]

PINKSTON, WILLIAM, a merchant in Donaghadie, was admitted as a burgess of Glasgow on 12 September 1707. [GBR]

PINKSTON, WILLIAM, the younger, a merchant in Donaghadie, was admitted as a burgess of Glasgow on 12 September 1707. [GBR]

PITCAIRN, PATRICK, was appointed Clerk of the Council of Connaught on 3 December 1612. [CSPIre]

PITTALLO, JOHN, master of the John of Glenarme arrived in Glasgow on 9 June 1666 from Carrickfergus. [NAS.E72.10.1]

POAG, JOHN, master of the Roebuck of Ardkleo arrived in Glasgow on 10 May 1689 from Dublin. [NAS.E72.19.14]

POLLOCK, JOHN, son of John Pollock in Ireland, was apprenticed to John Wilson, a barber in Edinburgh, on 16 June 1708. [REA]

POLLOCK, WILLIAM, a Lieutenant of the Londonderry Regiment of Foot in 1689. [DAL.III.83]

POLLOK, JOHN, a Scots-Irish student at Glasgow University in 1702. [MUG#174]

POLLOK, JOHN, a gentleman in Dublin, 1704. [NAS.Argyll Sheriff Court Book #III, 224.11.1705]

PORTER, JAMES, a merchant, eldest son of Hew Porter in Lochlerne, Ireland, was admitted as a burgess of Irvine on 26 May 1665. [MRBI#171]

PORTER, JOHN, a Scots-Irish student at Glasgow University in 1703. [MUG#177]

PORTER, THOMAS, master of the Nightingale of Belfast arrived in Glasgow on 16 February 1686 from Dublin. [NAS.E72.19.12]

PORTER, WILLIAM, a Scots-Irish student at Glasgow University in 1703. [MUG#177]

PRESTON, DAVID, quartermaster to the Earl of Dunbarton's Regiment at Kinsale in April 1679. [HMC.Ormonde.II.220]

PRESTON, JOHN, Captain of the Earl of Dunbarton's Regiment at Kinsale in April 1679. [HMC.Ormonde.II.219]

PRINGLE, WILLIAM, master and merchant of the barque Nightingale of Belfast arrived in Ayr on 11 June 1681 from Belfast; also arrived in Port Glasgow on 2 August 1681 from Belfast, from Port Glasgow bound for Belfast in August 1681; from Glasgow to Belfast on 1 July 1686. [NAS.E72.3.5; E72.19.3/4]

QUEEN, ROBERT, a currier, to Ireland in 1696. [NAS.CH2.537.15.1/158]

RAE, ARCHIBALD, merchant of the Elizabeth of Portavadie arrived in the Clyde in December 1695 from Belfast. [NAS.E72.19.23]

RAE, JANET, a Protestant refugee from Ireland, 1689. [NAS.CH2.537.15.1/13-29]

RAINEY, ROBERT, a Scots-Irish student at Glasgow University in 1699. [MUG#167]

RAMSAY, DAVID, son of Alexander Ramsay a mariner in Strabane, who was apprenticed with George Childers, a saddler in Edinburgh on 24 August 1664. [REA]

RAMSAY, GILBERT, moderator of the Presbytery of Carrickfergus, 1649. [GA#276]

RAMSAY, HUGH, a Scots-Irish student at Glasgow University in 1700. [MUG#168]

RAMSAY, MATTHEW, master of the Margaret of Coleraine, arrived in Glasgow on 26 February 1684 from Coleraine. [NAS.E72.19.9]

RAMSAY, MATTHEW, a Scots-Irish student at Glasgow University in 1705. [MUG#182]

RANKIN, ALEXANDER, a defender at the Siege of Derry, 29 July 1689. [WDSD]

RANKIN, HUGH, a burgess of Rathmullen, County Donegal, 18 November 1612. [CSPIre.Carte pp62/87]

RANKIN, JAMES, master of the Janet of Belfast, arrived in the Clyde on 8 June 1691. [NAS.E72.19.21]

RANKIN, WILLIAM, Provost of Rathmullen, County Donegal, 18 November 1612. [CSPIre.Carte pp62/87]

RATCLIFFE, ALEXANDER, a defender at the Siege of Derry, 29 July 1689. [WDSD]

REED, ALEXANDER, a Scots-Irish student at Glasgow University in 1703. [MUG#176]

REID, COLIN, in Tullyhogue, County Tyrone, 1610. [Tullyhogue Muster Roll]

REID, DAVID, master of the Jean of Donaghadie arrived in the Clyde from Donaghadie in January 1696. [NAS.E72.19.23]

REID, JAMES, from Loch Larne, Ireland, to Saltcoats, Ayrshire, in 1686. [RPCS.XII.378]

REID, JAMES, master of the Jane of Portaferry arrived in Glasgow on 23 June 1686 from Dublin. [NAS.E72.19.12]

REID, MALCOLM, a burgess of Donegal, 20 October 1612. [CSPIre.Carte pp.62/120]

REID, ROBERT, a Scots-Irish student at Glasgow University in 1699. [MUG#167]

REID, WILLIAM, master and merchant of the William of Portaferry from Irvine to Ireland on 20 July 1681. [NAS.E72.12.3]

REYNOLD, JAMES, Strabane Muster Roll of 1630. [PRONI#T808/15164]

RICHARDSON, EDWARD, 1690. [PRONI#T729/2/8]

RICHARDSON, ELIZABETH, 1694-1736. [PRONI#T448/75]

RICHARDSON, JOHN, 1663. [PRONI#D689/96, etc]

RICHARDSON, JOHN, a Scots-Irish student at Glasgow University in 1702. [MUG#174]

RITCHY, JOHN, a Scots-Irish student at Glasgow University in 1703. [MUG#177]

ROBERTSON, GEORGE, merchant on the James of Belfast arrived in the Clyde on 5 November 1695 from Belfast. [NAS.E72.19.23]

ROBISON, ALEXANDER, from Ireland, in Penningham in 1714. [Penningham KSR:10.2.1714]

ROBISON, CUTHBERT, a merchant, who was admitted as a burgess and guilds-brother of Glasgow by the right of his wife Janet, daughter of Constantine Miller and wright burgess and guilds-brother, on 25 December 1622 but had moved to Ireland by 1655. [GBR]

ROBISON, JOHN, merchant on the Jean of Hollywood arrived in Irvine on 26 June 1669 from Belfast. [NAS.E72.12.1]

ROBISON, WILLIAM, Cornet of the Royal Regiment of Dragoons of Ireland, was admitted as a burgess and guilds-brother of Glasgow on 31 October 1716. [GBR]

RODGER, JOHN, master of the Margaret of Larne arrived in Glasgow on 28 September 1672 from Carrickfergus. [NAS.E72.10.3]

RODGER, JOHN, a Scots-Irish student at Glasgow University in 1702. [MUG#174]

RODGER, JOHN, master of the Brunswick of Londonderry, a galley, from Port Glasgow to Jamaica in October 1716, [NAS.E508.10.6]

ROE, WILLIAM, a Scots-Irish student at Glasgow University in 1702. [MUG#175]

ROLLO, ARCHIBALD, Captain of the Earl of Dunbarton's Regiment at Kinsale in April 1679. [HMC.Ormonde.II.219]

RONNALD, PAUL, of Killileaghe, County Down, 1637. [ECA.Moses.18/725]

ROODIE, THOMAS, merchant of the Good Fortune of Donaghadie at Port Patrick on 1 November 1681. [NAS.E72.20.7]

ROSE, WILLIAM, an Ensign of Mountjoy's Regiment of Foot in 1701. [DAL.IV.259]

ROSS, ANDREW, master of the Katherine of Belfast at the port of Stranraer in November 1715, [NAS.E508.9.6]

ROSS, CHARLES, a Captain of the Inniskilling Dragoons in 1689, and by 16 July 1695 reached the rank of Colonel of the Regiment. [DAL.III.34]

ROSS, FRANCIS, a Scots-Irish student at Glasgow University in 1702. [MUG#173]

ROSS, WILLIAM, Captain of Foot in HM Army in Ireland 18 November 1667. [HMC.Ormonde#II, 194]

ROSS, ..., of Portencaple, in Ireland, 1691. [RPCS.XVI.281]

ROSSUDIR, NICOLAS, a seaman from Washford, a prisoner in Greenock, to be exchanged for a Scot in Irish hands, 1642. [RPCS.VII.339]

ROWAN, ROBERT, 2nd Lieutenant of Mountjoy's Regiment of Foot, 1694, 1701. [DAL.III.391; IV.259]

ROWAND, WILLIAM, reimbursed fifty shillings sterling by Glasgow burgh council for taking an orphan to Ireland, on 31 August 1661. [GBR]

RUDLIE, GEORGE, an Irishman who was captured in Kirkcudbright and imprisoned in Edinburgh Tolbooth during 1641. [RPCS.VII.210/221]

RUTHERFORD, THOMAS, Ensign of the Earl of Dunbarton's Regiment at Kinsale in April 1679. [HMC.Ormonde.II.219]

RUTHVEN, JOHN, Lieutenant of the Earl of Dunbarton's Regiment at Kinsale in April 1679. [HMC.Ormonde.II.219]

RYND, DAVID, eldest son of David Rynd of Enniskillen and his wife Margaret Irvine, a Captain of the Inniskilling Regiment of Foot, at Dundalk in October 1689. [DAL.III.122]

SAMPLE, WILLIAM, a Lieutenant of a Regiment of Foot in Longford, Leinster, 1680. [HMC.Ormonde.II.222]

SANDERSON, Captain ALEXANDER, of Tillelagan, County Tyrone, 26 January 1678. [NAS.GD109.1009-1010]

SANDERSON, ALEXANDER, a defender at the Siege of Derry, 29 July 1689. [WDSD]; Captain of a Londonderry or Inniskilling Regiment in 1690. [DAL.III.168]

SANDERSON, ALEXANDER, 1726. [PRONI#T1859/3]

SANDERSON, JAMES, in Tullyhogue, County Tyrone, 1610. [Tullyhogue Muster Roll]

SANDERSON, JAMES, 1680. [PRONI#T1859/2]

SANDERSON, Lieutenant Colonel ROBERT, in Antrim, 1645. [CSPIre.#CCLX]

SANDERSON, Colonel ROBERT, Castle Sanderson, 1711. [NAS.GD406.1.5689]

SANDERSON, ROBERT, of Castle Sanderson, County Down, decree against Sir Humphrey Colquhoun of Luss dated 15 February 1710. [ECA.Moses.140/5476]

SANDERSON, ROBERT, 1723. [PRONI#T1075/37/20]

SANDERSON, WILLIAM, in Tullyhogue, County Tyrone, 1610. [Tullyhogue Muster Roll]

SANDILAND, ROBERT, a Scots-Irish student at Glasgow University in 1705. [MUG#182]

SANDIRSON, ALEXANDER, a Scottish soldier who fought in Flanders and Poland, settled in Ireland, justice of the peace and high sheriff, died 1633. [Desertcreat gravestone, County Tyrone]

SAUNDERSON, ALEXANDER, was granted letters patent of denization and lands in the precinct of Mountjoy, barony of Dungannon, County Tyrone – the manor of Saunderson – on 25 November 1630. [CPR#570]

SAUNDERSON, RICHARD, a burgess of Mountjoy, County Tyrone, 20 October 1612. [CSPIre.Carte pp.62/86]

SAVAGE, JAMES, an Irishman who was captured in Kirkcudbright and imprisoned in Edinburgh Tolbooth during 1641. [RPCS.VII.210/221]

SCOTT, ANDREW, Ensign of the Earl of Dunbarton's Regiment at Kinsale in April 1679. [HMC.Ormonde.II.219]

SCOTT, FRANCIS, a burgess of Agher, County Tyrone, 6 April 1613. [CSPIre#Carte pp62/101]

SCOTT, FRANCIS, 1st Lieutenant of the Earl of Donegal's Regiment of Foot in 1701. [DAL.IV.257]

SCOTT, GEORGE, from Ireland, in Penningham, 1713.
[Penningham KSR, 20.5.1713]

SCOTT, JAMES, master of the Margaret of Belfast arrived in Ayr
on 19 March 1673 from Belfast. [NAS.E72.3.3]

SCOTT, JOHN, Lieutenant of the Earl of Dunbarton's Regiment at
Kinsale in April 1679. [HMC.Ormonde.II.219]

SCOTT, JOHN, from Ireland to Dumfries in 1690.
[NAS.CH2.537.15.1/27]

SCOTT, MATTHEW, master of the James of Lochlarne from Port
Glasgow to Lochlarne on 1 July 1682; of the Elizabeth of
Belfast arrived in Glasgow on 2 March 1689 from Belfast;
and of the Prosperity of Belfast at Port Glasgow in January
1691. [NAS.E72.19.6/14/21]

SCOTT, RICHARD, a burgess of Agher, County Tyrone, 6 April
1613. [CSPIre#Carte pp62/101]

SCOTT, THOMAS, Lieutenant of the Earl of Dunbarton's
Regiment at Kinsale in April 1679. [HMC.Ormonde.II.219]

SCOTT, WILLIAM, Tullyhogue, County Tyrone, 1610.
[Tullyhogue Muster Roll]

SCOTT, WILLIAM, was appointed as Searcher and Gauger of the
port of Dublin 23 June 1626. [CPR#110]

SCOTT, WILLIAM, married Katherine Brown in Cramond,
Scotland, then he left for Ireland. She, later, assuming that he
was dead married James Reid in Dalmeny, however William
Scott returned from Ireland in 1642. [SLT#162]

SEATON, ALEXANDER, son of Sir John Seaton of Barns,
accused of assisting the Ferrells in Ireland, imprisoned in
Dublin, later imprisoned in Edinburgh Tolbooth, in 1642.
[RPCS.VII.339]

SEATON, CHRISTOPHER, rector of Magherynecrosse, 1631.
[CPR#593]

SEMPLE, Sir JAMES, granted lands formerly held by Sir James Fullerton, 16 August 1614. [CSPIre#Docquet Book]

SERVIT, JANET, formerly married to John Hunter a joiner, then wife of John Campbell of Ballycastle, County Antrim, see deposition at Coleraine on 9 February 1652. [ISC.I.283]

SHARP, CHRISTIAN, widow of Peter Sharp a preacher at Drumbo, fled to Scotland by 1642. [SLT#150]

SHAW, CHARLES, a Captain of the Londonderry Regiment of Foot in 1689. [DAL.III.83]

SHAW, HENRY, a Captain of the Londonderry Regiment of Foot in 1689. [DAL.III.83]

SHAW, HEW, merchant on the Elizabeth of Londonderry which arrived in the Clyde in April 1691 from Londonderry. [NAS.E72.19.21]

SHAW, JAMES, Market Hill, County Armagh, see deposition dated 14 August 1643. [ISC.I.197]

SHAW, JAMES, a landowner in the parish of Glenarme and the parish of Layde, barony of Glenarme, in 1660. [MA#466]

SHAW, JOHN, a proprietor in the parish of Carncastle, barony of Glencarn, 1641. [MA#457]

SHAW, PATRICK, a burgess of Newton Ards, County Down, 17 January 1612. [CSPIre.Carte pp62/84]

SHAW, WILLIAM, a Captain of the Londonderry Regiment of Foot in 1689. [DAL.III.83]

SHAW, WILLIAM, a Lieutenant of the Londonderry Regiment of Foot in 1689. [DAL.III.83]

SHEARER, JAMES, master of the Recovery of Donaghadie at Port Patrick on 20 October 1682; also in Port Glasgow in December 1695. [NAS.E72.20.7; E72.19.23]

SHEARER, ROBERT, master of the William of Belfast at Port Glasgow in October 1689. [NAS.E72.19.14]

SHEEN, FRANCIS, a Scots-Irish student at Glasgow University in 1704. [MUG#180]

SHIELLS, ..., a Scot, was despatched by Edward Chichester in Belfast to Edinburgh on 24 October 1641. [APS.V.ii.appx.688]

SIMPSON, EDWARD, a landowner in the parish of Maghrasharkan, barony of Killenway, 1660. [MA#466]

SIMPSON, JANET, wife of Alexander Seton in Hillsborough, Ireland, and only daughter and heir of William Simpson a gardener in Erskine, an Instrument of Sasine dated 3 March 1705. [ECA.Moses.176/6941]

SINCLAIR, JAMES, Tullyhogue, County Tyrone, 1610. [Tullyhogue Muster Roll]

SINCLAIR, Reverend JOHN, born around 1640, minister of Leckpatrick and of Camus-juxta-Mourne, parish of Strabane, from 1660s, married (2) Anna Galbraith, died in March 1702, father of Elizabeth, Ezachial, John, William, Anne, Elizabeth, Andrew and Rebecca. [Leckpatrick gravestone]

SINCLAIR, JOHN, from Ireland, in Penningham in 1714. [Penningham KSR:10.2.1714]

SINCLAIR, ROBERT, in Strabane, was admitted a burgess and guildsbrother of Ayr on 3 July 1676. [Ayr Burgess Roll]

SINCLAIR, ROBERT, merchant of the Lewis of Belfast arrived in the Clyde in October 1695 from Belfast. [NAS.E72.19.23]

SINCLAIR, Sir WILLIAM, lands held in King's County were transferred to Viscount Baltinglass on 4 July 1628. [CPR#330]

SKIPPON, SAMUEL, an Anglo-Irish student at Glasgow University in 1702. [MUG#175]

SMALL, ALEXANDER, in the parish of Finvoy, 1698.
[RGSU#32]

SMITH, BENJAMIN, a Scots-Irish student at Glasgow University
in 1701. [MUG#172]

SMITH, DAVID, master of the William and David of Belfast from
there to Port Glasgow in July 1690. [NAS.E72.19.16]

SMITH, HENRY, merchant of the Merchant of Larne from Irvine
to Belfast on 13 January 1682; and of the Anna of Belfast
arrived in the Clyde from Dublin in January 1696.
[NAS.E72.19.23; E72.12.6]

SMITH, WILLIAM, alderman of Belfast, his niece Mrs Margaret
Binnie and his factor baillie John Ballantyne, a merchant of
Ayr, 1702. [ECA.Moses 163/6297]

SMITH, WILLIAM, a Scots-Irish student at Glasgow University in
1703. [MUG#177]

SMITH, WILLIAM, a minister in Balla, Ireland, was admitted as a
burgess and guilds-brother of Glasgow on 6 June 1715.
[GBR]

SOMERVELL, WILLIAM, a barber in Dublin, was admitted as a
burgess and guilds-brother of Glasgow on 1 August 1717.
[GBR]

SOMERVILLE, JAMES, with a sword, Tullyhogue, County
Tyrone, 1610. [Tullyhogue Muster Roll]

SOMERVILLE, JOHN, with a sword and pike, Tullyhogue,
County Tyrone, 1610. [Tullyhogue Muster Roll]

SPEARS, WILLIAM, master of the Salmon of Belfast from Port
Glasgow to Belfast in October 1689. [NAS.E72.19.15]

SPENCE, JAMES, minister at Castle Martyr, Ireland, son of
Reverend Alexander Spence in Birnie, Morayshire, ca.1710.
[NAS.RS29.V194]

SPOTSWOOD, Sir HENRY, purchased lands in County Tyrone on 28 September 1629. [CPR#516]

SPOTSWOOD, Sir HENRY, late of Drumboate, County Monaghan, see deposition dated 15 January 1641. [ISC.II.163]

SPOTSWOOD, Sir JOHN, was granted lands in County Leitrim on 25 May 1625. [CPR#34]

STALKER, WILLIAM, master of the Recovery of Coleraine from Port Glasgow to Londonderry, in April 1690. [NAS.E72.19.19]

STEDMAN, HENRY, Lieutenant of a Regiment of Guards in Ireland, 22 August 1677. [HMC. Ormonde#II.206]

STEELE, JAMES, a cooper in the Grange, near Toome, County Antrim, 1641, see deposition dated 14 March 1652. [ISC.I.286]

STEELE, ROBERT, in Tullyhogue, County Tyrone, 1610. [Tullyhogue Muster Roll]

STEELE, WILLIAM, in Tullyhogue, County Tyrone, 1610. [Tulluhogue Muster Roll]

STEENE, SYLVESTER, possibly master of a ship of Leith at Waterford in September 1601. [CSPIre.#CCIX/105]

STEUART, ROBERT OGE, gentleman in the parish of Culfaghtrim, see deposition dated 4 March 1652. [ISC.I.249]

STEUART, Sir ROBERT, Captain of Foot in HM Army in Ireland 18 November 1667. [HMC.Ormonde#II, 194]

STEUART, THOMAS, Captain of Foot in HM Army in Ireland 18 November 1667. [HMC.Ormonde#II, 194]

STEUART, WILLIAM, Colonel of the Royal Regiment of Scots Horse in Ireland around 1689. [CTP.XVII.6.1.1692]

STEVEN, DAVID, from Ireland, in Penningham in November 1707. [Penningham KSR, 11.11.1707]

STEVENSON, JAMES, soldier of Colonel Bayly's Company in February 1648. [HMC.Ormonde.II.70]

STEVENSON, JAMES, a Scots-Irish student at Glasgow University in 1703. [MUG#178]

STEVENSON, MARMADUKE, a Scots-Irish student at Glasgow University in 1700. [MUG#169]

STEVENSON, WILLIAM, a burgess of Strabane, County Tyrone, 25 November 1612. [CSPIre#Carte.pp62/117]

STEWART, AGNES, born in Mochrum, Wigtownshire, moved to Ireland, arrived in Penningham parish 'with child' in April 1706, encouraged and agreed to return to Mochrum. [Penningham KSR, 14.4.1706]

STEWART, ALEXANDER, a debtor in Ireland of Lord Antrim in 1638. [MA#476]

STEWART, ALEXANDER, a defender at the Siege of Derry, 29 July 1689. [WDSD]

STEWART, ALEXANDER, Lieutenant of Mountjoy's Regiment of Foot, 1694. [DAL.III.391]

STEWART, ALEXANDER, a saddler in Coleraine, and his wife Isobel Campbell, daughter of Duncan Campbell of Elister and his wife Elizabeth, marriage contract dated 18 June 1706. [NAS.Argyll Sheriff Court Book #VI, 4.3.1720]

STEWART, ALEXANDER, a Captain of the Irish Dragoons in 1693. [DAL.III.300]

STEWART, ALEXANDER, from Ireland to Dumfries in 1690. [NAS.CH2.537.15.1/64-69]

STEWART, ANDREW, 3rd Baron Ochiltree, 1560-1629. [PRONI#T530/5]

STEWART, ANDREW, Lord Castlestewart, County Tyrone, was admitted as a baronet of Nova Scotia on 2 October 1628. [NAS.BNS#62]

STEWART, Sir ANDREW, was granted letters patent of denization and the manors of Castlestewart and of Foreward, on 26 February 1630. [CPR#533]

STEWART, ANDREW, 3rd Baron Castle Stuart, 1680. [PRONI#DA173/291]

STEWART, ANNA, widow of John Mader the minister of Donochmoir who was killed by rebels in Ireland during 1641, fled with her six children to Scotland by 1642. [SLT#149]

STEWART, ARCHIBALD, Lord Antrim's principal agent from 1630 to 1665, and a leaseholder in Ballylough near Bushmills, and in Ballintoy. [MA#438]

STEWART, ARCHIBALD, of Ballintaylor, parish of Billy, barony of Carie, 1641. [MA#457]

STEWART, ARCHIBALD, in Coleraine, 1642. [NAS.GD406/1/1307]

STEWART, ARCHIBALD, of Ballintoy, Ireland, 1665. [Rothesay Town Council Records, 19.10.1665]

STEWART, ARTHUR, Captain of Mountjoy's Regiment of Foot, 1694, 1701. [DAL.III.391/259]

STEWART, BARBARA, fled from Ireland to Scotland in 1642. [SLT#143]

STEWART, BLACK JOHN, from Ireland, in Kingarth on 25 February 1683. [Kingarth Kirk Session Records, 22.4.1683]

STEWART, CHARLES, Captain of Mountjoy's Regiment of Foot, 1694, 1702. [DAL.III.391; IV.277]

STEWART, CHARLES, Ensign of Mountjoy's Regiment of Foot, 1694, 1701. [DAL.III.391; IV.259]

STEWART, CHARLES, a Scots-Irish student at Glasgow University in 1698. [MUG#164]

STEWART, DAVID, a burgess of Clogher, 12 December 1612. [CSPIre.Carte pp62/77]

STEWART, GEORGE, a burgess of Clogher, 12 December 1612. [CSPIre.Carte pp62/77]

STEWART, GEORGE, Lieutenant of the Earl of Dunbarton's Regiment at Kinsale in April 1679. [HMC.Ormonde.II.219]

STEWART, GEORGE, from Ireland, in Penningham in 1712. [Penningham KSR:13.2.1712]

STEWART, GRISSEL, fled from Ireland to Scotland in 1642. [SLT#143]

STEWART, HENRY, was granted letters patent of denization and granted the manor of Carragan in County Tyrone, on 3 March 1630. [CPR#530]

STEWART, HENRY, petitioned the Scots Parliament for losses incurred by him in Ireland, 1641. [APS.V.431]

STEWART, HUMPHREY, born around 1613, see deposition dated 3 May 1653. [ISC.II.22]

STEWART, JAMES, son of John Stewart of Ballinstraid, County Antrim, heir to his uncle Ninian Stewart the elder of Kilcattan, 1666. [NAS.Argyll Sasines #1273]

STEWART, JAMES, Lieutenant of the Earl of Dunbarton's Regiment at Kinsale in April 1679. [HMC.Ormonde.II.219]

STEWART, JAMES, in Ballintoy, Ireland, deceased, father of Finuell, Margaret, Isobel, Janet and Grissall, also Mary, wife of James Johnstone a cooper in Rothesay, 1687. [Rothesay Town Council Records, 10.1687]

STEWART, JAMES, merchant in Belfast, petitioned the Scots Parliament in 1689. [APS.IX.49]

STEWART, JAMES, Ensign of Mountjoy's Regiment of Foot, 1694; was appointed Captain-Lieutenant of the same regiment on 1 April 1697. [DAL.III.391; IV.191/259]

STEWART, JAMES, a Scots-Irish student at Glasgow University in 1701. [MUG#172]

STEWART, JOHN, was granted letters patent of denization and granted the manor of Stewartscourt in County Donegal on 9 May 1629. [CPR#453]

STEWART, JOHN OGE, leaseholder of Ballyloiske in the Grange of Drumtullagh, 10 March 1611. [MA#439]

STEWART, JOHN, in Ballmenoch, Ireland, heir to Walter Stewart, burgess of Rothesay, 1676. [Rothesay Town Council Records, 28.6.1676]

STEWART, JOHN, in Glenluchock, fled to Ireland in 1684. [Penningham KSR, 19.2.1711]

STEWART, JOHN, from Rothesay to Ireland in 1695. [Rothesay KSR, 19.8.1695]

STEWART, JOHN, from Ireland, in Minnigaff parish on 15 January 1721. [Minnigaff Kirk Session Records, 15.1.1721]

STEWART, KATHERINE, daughter of Sir William Stewart, wife of Sir James Montgomery, parents of one son, died in February 1634. [Newtonstewart gravestone]

STEWART, KATHERINE, from Ireland, in Penningham in 1714. [Penningham KSR:10.2.1714]

STEWART, LUDOVICK, a burgess of Clogher, 12 December 1612. [CSPIre.Carte pp62/77]

STEWART, MARMADUKE, a defender at the Siege of Derry, 29 July 1689. [WDSD]

STEWART, PATRICK, from Ireland, in Kingarth in 1693. [Kingarth Kirk Session Records, 12.3.1693]

STEWART, Colonel ROBERT, in Antrim, 1645. [CSPIre.#CCLX]

STEWART, Sir ROBERT, 1664. [PRONI#t545/4]

STEWART, ROBERT, son of James Stewart in Ballintoy, Ireland, 1672, 1686. [Rothesay Town Council Records, 24.1.1672; 2.11.1686]

STEWART, ROBERT, a former collector in Kingarth, moved to Ireland by January 1681. [Kingarth Kirk Session Records, 23.1.1681]

STEWART, ROBERT, a tenant farmer in Temple Currdie, Ireland, 26 July 1714. [NAS.GD97.Sec.1/626]

STEWART, SAMUEL, Lieutenant of Life Guards, Ireland, 22 March 1675, quartered in Armagh in August 1677, at Drogheda 25 December 1678. [HMC.Ormonde#II/202, 206, 214]

STEWART, THOMAS, a land laborer from County Donegal, from Loch Larne, Ireland, to Saltcoats, Ayrshire, in 1686. [RPCS.XII.378]

STEWART, WILLIAM, Captain of Foot at Dundalk, 5 November 1608. [CSPIre#CCXXV]

STEWART, WILLIAM, in Ireland, petitioned the Scots Parliament, 1639. [APS.V.268]

STEWART, Captain WILLIAM, petitioned the Scots Parliament for losses incurred by him and his father Harry Stewart of Cougan in Ireland, 1641. [APS.V.487; V.ii.423]

STEWART, Captain WILLIAM, son of Lord Garlies, was killed at Kilcullin Bridge in 1641. [Drumbeg gravestone, County Down]

STEWART, WILLIAM, born in Whithorn, Wigtownshire, son of Archibald Stewart, settled in County Tyrone by 1643. [MA#75]

STEWART, WILLIAM, pardoned for the murder of George Russell on 18 July 1628, but sentenced to be burnt on the hand. [CPR#329]

STEWART, Sir WILLIAM, granted letters patent of denization also lands in County Tyrone – the manor of Mount Stewart – on 26 July 1629. [CPR#477]

STEWART, Sir WILLIAM, Colonel of a Regiment of Guards in Ireland 22 August 1677, in Dublin July 1680. [HMC.Ormonde#II, 206, 222]

STEWART, WILLIAM, a defender at the Siege of Derry, 29 July 1689. [WDSD]

STEWART, WILLIAM, of Ballylaune, was appointed Major of Brigadier Stewart's Regiment on 27 July 1691. [DAL.III.217]

STEWART, WILLIAM, 1st Lieutenant of Mountjoy's Regiment of Foot, 1694, 1701. [DAL.III.391/259]

STINSON, ROBERT, master and merchant of the Providence of Belfast arrived in Irvine on 14 August 1669 from Belfast. [NAS.E72.12.1]

STIRLING, HENRY, Ensign of the Earl of Donegal's Regiment of Foot, 16 February 1695, 1700. [DAL.IV.103/257]

STIRLING, HENRY, Ensign of the Earl of Donegal's Regiment in 1702. [DAL.IV.276]

STIRLING, JAMES, Captain of the Earl of Donegal's Regiment in 1702. [DAL.IV.276]

STIRLING, JOHN, Lieutenant of the Earl of Dunbarton's Regiment at Kinsale in April 1679. [HMC.Ormonde.II.219]

STIRLING, JOHN, merchant of the Elizabeth of Donaghadie arrived in the Clyde in October 1696 from Belfast. [NAS.E72.19.23]

STIRLING, ROBERT, Lieutenant of the Inniskilling Regiment of Foot in 1691, killed at the Siege of Limerick. [DAL.III.206/218]

STIRLING, WILLIAM, a prisoner in Kilkenny, December 1647. [CSP.Domestic. Interegnum. E26/123]

STOT, ALEXANDER, master of the ....of Balliwalter at Port Patrick on 4 November 1682. [NAS.E72.20.8]

STRACHAN, ALEXANDER, soldier of Colonel Bayly's Company in February 1648. [HMC.Ormonde.II.70]

STRACHAN, THOMAS, merchant of the James of Portaferry arrived in the Clyde from Belfast in October 1695. [NAS.E72.19.23]

STRANG, WILLIAM, minister at Athalie, Ireland, and his wife Christian, disposition dated 16 August 1637. [ECA.Moses.18/738; 19/773]

STUART, Colonel Sir ROBERT, in Belfast, 1647. [CSPIre.#CCLXIII]

STUART, Captain WILLIAM, a landowner in the parish of Layde, barony of Glenarme. 1660. [MA#466]

STURGEON, ROBERT, a Scots-Irish student at Glasgow University in 1703. [MUG#177]

SUMMERS, HENRY, master of the Mary of Belfast arrived in Glasgow on 28 May 1689 from Belfast. [NAS.E72.19.14]

SUTHY, HENRY, a Scots-Irish student at Glasgow University in 1701. [MUG#171]

SYMMER, MARGARET, mother-in-law of John Campbell in Galston, and relict of John Campbell a minister at Lochbricklay, Ireland, around 1710. [NAS.GD253.136.14]

TAIT, JAMES, a Scots-Irish student at Glasgow University in 1698. [MUG#166]

TAIT, MARGARET, fled from Minnigaff to Ireland in 1720. [Minnigaff Kirk Session Records, 9 June 1720]

TAYLOR, GILBERT, an Irish student at Glasgow University in 1702. [MUG#173]

TAYLOR, JAMES, merchant of the George of Coleraine arrived in the Clyde from Coleraine on 5 November 1696. [NAS.E72.19.23]

TAYLOR, WILLIAM, a Scots-Irish student at Glasgow University in 1705. [MUG#182]

TEMPLETON, ALAN, a Scots-Irish student at Glasgow University in 1701. [MUG#171]

TEMPLETON, JOHN, master of the Isiah of the Isle of McGee, arrived in Ayr during May 1673 from Ireland. [NAS.E72.3.3]

THOMPSON, DAVID, in Tullyhogue, County Tyrone, 1610. [Tullyhogue Muster Roll]

THOMPSON, LOUIS, a merchant in Belfast, 1691. [RPCS.XVI.309]

THOMPSON, WILLIAM, a passenger in the Providence of Irvine arrived in Ayr on 15 July 1673 from Belfast. [NAS.E72.3.3]

THOMPSON, WILLIAM, Lieutenant of the Earl of Dunbarton's Regiment at Kinsale in April 1679. [HMC.Ormonde.II.219]

THOMSON, HUGH, a merchant burgess of Londonderry, husband of Elizabeth Erskine, 1620. [Argyll Sasines#1/126-127]

THOMSON, JAMES, a Scots-Irish student at Glasgow University in 1702. [MUG#175]

THOMSON, LOUIS, a merchant in Belfast, 1689. [RPCS.XVI.310]

THOMSON, WILLIAM, in Kirkgunzeon, accused of adultery, fled to Ireland in 1691. [NAS.CH2.537.15.2/85-197]

THOMSON, WILLIAM, an Irish student at Glasgow University in 1705. [MUG#182]

TREWMAN, JOHN, died in Ireland by 1641. [SLT#121]

TROTTER, ELIZABETH, from Ireland to Dumfries in 1690. [NAS.CH2.537.15.1/30, 61]

TROTTER, FRANCIS, killed by rebels at Tully Castle, County Fermanagh, on 25 December 1641. See Patrick Hume's deposition. [ISC.I.215]

TROTTER, THOMAS, killed by rebels at Tully Castle, County Fermanagh, on 25 December 1641. See Patrick Hume's deposition. [ISC.I.215]

TULLOS, ..., a proprietor in the parish of Carncastle, barony of Glencarn, 1641. [MA#457]

TUMELTY, JAMES, master of the James of Portaferry arrived in the Clyde from Belfast in October 1695. [NAS.E72.19.23]

TURNER, WILLIAM, son of Robert Turner, sometime in Ireland now in Edinburgh, was apprenticed to Gavin Weir a merchant in Edinburgh on 23 August 1643. [REA]

TWEEDY, PATRICK, a Lieutenant at Carrickfergus, 25 December 1678. [HMC.Ormonde.II, 214]

URIE, DAVID, a Scots-Irish student at Glasgow University in 1701. [MUG#172]

VERNOR, ANDREW, son of John Vernor in Ireland, was apprenticed to Andrew Vernor a merchant in Edinburgh on 3 April 1661. [REA]

VERNOR, BENJAMIN, from Ireland, in Penningham in 1714.[Penningham KSR:10.2.1714]

VILLARS, Mrs, from Ireland, in Penningham on 19 November 1708. [Penningham KSR, 19.11.1708]

WALKER, ALEXANDER, master of the Catherine of Coleraine, from Glasgow on 25 November 1684 bound for Coleraine. [NAS.E72.19.9]

WALKER, GEORGE, in Londonderry, 1689. [NAS.GD406.1.3527][WDSD]

WALKER, GEORGE, Colonel of a Londonderry Volunteer Regiment in 1689. [DAL.III.308]

WALKER, JAMES, in Tullyhogue, County Tyrone, 1610. [Tullyhogue Muster Roll]

WALKER, JOHN, a Scots-Irish student at Glasgow University in 1703. [MUG#177]

WALKER, ROBERT, a Scots-Irish student at Glasgow University in 1700. [MUG#168]

WALLACE, ALEXANDER, pipe major of the Earl of Dunbarton's Regiment at Kinsale in April 1679. [HMC.Ormonde#II,220]

WALLACE, HUGH, a Scots-Irish student at Glasgow University in 1705. [MUG#182]

WALLACE, JOHN, granted a commission 3 March 1630. [CPR#572]

WALLACE, JONATHAN, a Captain of the Inniskilling Regiment of Foot, at Dundalk in October 1689. [DAL.III.121/206]

WALLACE, ROBERT, from Kingarth, in Ireland in 1649. [Kingarth Kirk Session Records, 28.1.1649]

WALLACE, ROBERT, a defender at the Siege of Derry, 29 July 1689. [WDSD]

WALLACE, ROBERT, born in Ballentpy, Ireland, settled in Rothesay in 1712. [Rothesay KSR, 12.11.1712]

WALLACE, SAMUEL, a Scots-Irish student at Glasgow University in 1702. [MUG#174]

WALLACE, WILLIAM, merchant of the <u>John of Londonderry</u> arrived in Port Glasgow on 17 September 1691 from Virginia. [NAS.E72.19.21]

WALLACE, WILLIAM, messenger, 1709. [NAS.NRAS#2522/CA3/19]

WALLACE, Mrs, a widow and a debtor in Ireland of Lord Antrim in 1638. [MA#476]

WALLACE, ..., master and merchant of the <u>John of Larne</u> at the port of Irvine on 26 April 1669. [NAS.E72.12.1]

WALLIS, JOHN, Strabane Muster Roll of 1630. [PRONI#T808/15164]

WALLIS, JOHN, Adjutant and Quartermaster of the Earl of Donegal's Regiment of Foot in 1701. [DAL.IV.257]

WALLS, JOHN, with a sword and snaphance, Tullyhogue, County Tyrone, 1610. [Muster Roll of Tullyhogue]

WALLS, JOHN, in Tullyhogue, County Tyrone, 1610. [Tullyhogue Muster Roll]

WALLS, JOHN, married **Isobel Wright** in an Episcopal church in England, from Troqueer parish, Dumfries-shire, to Ireland in 1699. [NAS.CH2.1036.1/19-20]

WALLS, KATHARINE, an old woman from Ireland, 1689. [NAS.CH2.537.15.1/18]

WARDEN, JOHN, master of the <u>Janet of Holywood</u> arrived in Glasgow on 27 April 1672 from Belfast. [NAS.E72.10.3]

WARDEN, WILLIAM, master of the <u>Jean of Hollywood</u> arrived in Irvine on 26 June 1669 from Belfast. [NAS.E72.12.1]

WATSON, ALEXANDER, Captain of a Londonderry or Inniskilling Regiment in 1690. [DAL.III.168]

WATSON, ANDREW, Captain of the Inniskilling Regiment of Foot in 1691. [DAL.III.206]

WATSON, DOROTHY, widow of Oliver Kennedy who was killed by rebels in 1641, with her eight children, fled to Scotland by 1642. [SLT#149]

WATT, RICHARD, a Scots-Irish student at Glasgow University in 1702. [MUG#175]

WATTS, WILLIAM, a merchant in Dublin, 1666. [NAS.RH9.5.11]

WAUCHOPE, COLLIN, of Kilkeel, son of James Wauchope and Helen Maxwell, born before 1614, a Captain in Sir James Montgomery's Regiment during the Irish Rebellion of 1641, died after 1682. [Wauchope Irish Pedigree]

WAUCHOPE, JAMES, born circa 1565, married Helen, daughter of William Maxwell of Newlands in 1598, settled in County Down around 1610, died before 1640. [Wauchope Irish Pedigree]

WAUCHOPE, JAMES, of Drumaghlish, born around 1616, son of James Wauchope and Helen Maxwell, married (2) Margaret daughter of Henry Maxwell of Finnabrogue, (2) in 1664 to Jean, daughter of Hugh Cochrane of Ardquin, died 1678. [Wauchope Irish Pedigree]

WAUCHOPE, WILLIAM, of Ballyclander, son of James Wauchope and Helen Maxwell, born before 1615, alive in 1663. [Wauchope Irish Pedigree]

WAUS, JOHN, rector of Kilmachernan, Ireland, at Ballichering, 1620. [Argyll Sasines #1/137]

WEDDELL, PATRICK, minister at Inniskillen for sixteen years, fled to Scotland in 1642. [SLT#151]

WEIR, JAMES, master of the Hanover of Belfast, a brigantine, from Port Glasgow to Barbados in September 1716, [NAS.E508.10.6]

WEIR, JOHN, absconded from Dumfries to Ireland in 1692. [NAS.CH2.537.15.2/145-146]

WEIR, THOMAS, Major of the Earl of Lanark's Regiment in Ireland, 1647. [APS.V.i.715]

WEIR, THOMAS, master of the Joan of Belfast from Port Glasgow to Madeira in January 1691. [NAS.E72.19.22]

WEIR, WILLIAM, from Irvine, Ayrshire, to Ireland by April 1681. [MRBI#292]

WELSH, WILLIAM, a hatmaker and feltmaker from Ireland, a Protestant refugee in Dumfries, 1689. [NAS.CH2.537.15.1/9-29]

WEMYSS, Sir PATRICK, Captain of Foot in HM Army in Ireland 18 November 1667. [HMC.Ormonde#II, 194]

WEST, JAMES, master of the barque Mullett of Londonderry arrived in Glasgow on 5 February 1689 from Londonderry. [NAS.E72.19.14]

WETHERINGTON, GEORGE, with a sword and snaphance, Tullyhogue, County Tyrone, 1610. [Muster Roll of Tullyhogue]

WHITE, MICHAEL, a merchant from Waterford, a prisoner in Greenock, to be exchanged for a Scot in Irish hands, 1642. [RPCS.VII.339]

WHITE, WILLIAM, Ensign of the Earl of Dunbarton's Regiment at Kinsale in April 1679. [HMC.Ormonde.II.219]

WIDDERSPOON, ALEXANDER, merchant of the Good Intention of Knock from Irvine to Carrickfergus on 18 July 1682. [NAS.E72.12.6]

WILLIAMSON, EDWARD, master of the Roebuck of Belfast arrived in the Clyde in August 1690 from Drogheda. [NAS.E72.19.18]

WILLIAMSON, GEORGE, master of the Salmon of Belfast, from Port Glasgow to Belfast in February 1688. [NAS.E72.19.15]

WILLIAMSON, JAMES, a burgess of Killileagh, 17 November 1612. [CSPIre#Carte pp62/110]

WILLIAMSON, JOHN, son of Robert Williamson in Coleraine, Ireland, was apprenticed to Archibald Wright a weaver in Edinburgh, on 20 July 1642. [REA]

WILLIAMSON, JOHN, an Anglo-Irish student at Glasgow University in 1702. [MUG#174]

WILLIAMSON, WILLIAM, a Scots-Irish student at Glasgow University in 1702. [MUG#174]

WILSON, FRANCIS, a defender at the Siege of Derry, 29 July 1689. [WDSD]

WILSON, JAMES, passenger on the Janet of McGee arrived in Ayr on 3 July 1673 from Ireland. [NAS.E72.3.3]

WILSON, JOHN, a burgess of Bangor, County Down, 25 November 1612. [CSPIre#Carte pp.62/117]

WILSON, JOHN, master of the Crystal of Donaghadie arrived in Irvine from Belfast on 24 June 1669. [NAS.E72.12.1]

WILSON, JOHN, master of the Speedwell of Glenarme arrived in Ayr on 27 July 1673 from Ireland; from Irvine to Ireland on 24 January 1681, also on 2 June 1681. [NAS.E72.3.3/6; E72.12.3]

WILSON, JOHN, an Ensign of the Londonderry Regiment of Foot in 1689. [DAL.III.83]

WILSON, JOHN, a Scots-Irish student at Glasgow University in 1704. [MUG#180]

WILSON, JOSEPH, an Ensign of the Londonderry Regiment of Foot in 1689. [DAL.III.83]

WILSON, MARGARET, from Ireland, 1703. [Penninghame Kirk Session Records, 13.8.1703]

WILSON, MARY, in Island McGee, 1641, se deposition.
[ISC.I.262]

WILSON, SAMUEL, master of the Plaindealing of Coleraine from
the Clyde to Madeira in January 1691. [NAS.E72.19.21]

WILSON, SAMUEL, a Scots-Irish student at Glasgow University
in 1702. [MUG#175]

WILSON, THOMAS, a Scots-Irish student at Glasgow University
in 1702. [MUG#175]

WILSON, THOMAS, a Scots-Irish student at Glasgow University
in 1704. [MUG#180]

WILSON, WILLIAM, a traveller in Ireland, was fined in the burgh
court of Irvine in 1601. [MRBI#241]

WILSON, WILLIAM, master of the Elizabeth of Donaghadie at
Port Patrick on 1 June 1683. [NAS.E72.20.8]

WINN, PETER, in Omagh, 1666. [Hearth Money Roll]

WIRLING, ROBERT, a Scots-Irish student at Glasgow University
in 1702. [MUG#174]

WOOD, HENRY, Strabane Muster Roll of 1630.
[PRONI#T808/15164]

WOOLLEY, RANDALL, master of the Adventure of Londonderry
arrived in Glasgow on 3 August 1667 from Londonderry.
[NAS.E72.10.1]

WORKMAN, ROBERT, master of the Elizabeth of Lochlarne,
arrived in Port Glasgow on 17 October 1682 from Dublin;
from Port Glasgow to Belfast on 8 November 1682.
[NAS.E72.19.5/8]

WRIGHT, JAMES, a Scots-Irish student at Glasgow University in
1703. [MUG#178]

WRIGHT, WALTER, Strabane Muster Roll of 1630.
[PRONI#T808/15164]

WYLLIE, JOHN, a burgess of Clogher, 12 December 1612. [CSPIre.Carte pp62/77]

WYLLIE, JOHN, master and merchant of the Margaret of Larne arrived in Irvine on 26 December 1668 from Larne, also on 2 November 1669. [NAS.E72.12.1]

WYLLIE, JOHN, from Ireland, 1703. [Penninghame Kirk Session Records, 13.8.1703]

YOUNG, ALEXANDER, master of the Alexander of Dublin, from the Clyde in December 1690 to Dublin. [NAS.E72.19.21]

YOUNG, JAMES, a defender at the Siege of Derry, 29 July 1689. [WDSD]

YOUNG, JOHN, was murdered near Lissan by rebels in 1641. [ISC.I.287]

YOUNG, JOHN, master of the Marie of Coleraine from Port Glasgow to Coleraine on 24 November 1681. [NAS.E72.19.6]

YOUNG, MATTHEW, from Ireland to Dumfries in 1690. [NAS.CH2.537.15.1/24]

YOUNG, ROBERT, a minister from Ireland, in Ayr during June 1688. [NAS.CH2.532.2.9]

YOUNG, SAMUEL, merchant of the Janet of Belfast, arrived in the Clyde on 8 June 1691. [NAS.E72.19.21]

YOUNGSON, JAMES, a Scots-Irish student at Glasgow University in 1705. [MUG#182]

SOME SHIPPING LINKS

ADVENTURE OF LEITH, **Malcolm McCalla,** arrived in Port
Glasgow on 21 September 1681 from Dublin.
[NAS.E72.19.3]

AGNES OF IRVINE, **Robert Stevenson,** from Dublin to Ayr in
October 1673. [NAS.E72.3.4]

AGNES OF AYR, arrived in Ayr on 21 May 1678 from Belfast.
[NAS.E72.3.4]

AGNES OF RENFREW, **Arthur Darleith,** from Port Glasgow to
Coleraine in April 1681, returned to Port Glasgow in May
1681. [NAS.E72.19.1]

AGNES OF GLASGOW, **John Miller,** arrived in Port Glasgow on
15 August 1681 from Carrickfergus. [NAS.E72.19.1]

AMITY OF GLASGOW, **James Wilson,** from Dundee to Ireland in
May 1681. [NAS.E72.7.6]

ANN OF AYR, from Ayr on 16 April 1681 to Belfast.
[NAS.E72.3.6]

ANNA AND HELEN OF IRVINE, **Robert Brown,** from Leith to
Belfast on 2 May 1691. [NAS.E72.15.44]

ANNE OF IRVINE, **Adam Cunningham,** arrived in Ayr from
Coleraine in October 1673. [NAS.E72.3.3]

BARBARA OF IRVINE, **William Martin,** from Dublin to Port
Glasgow in December 1683. [NAS.E72.19.9]

BLESSING OF AYR, arrived in Ayr on 26 February 1673 from
Belfast. [NAS.E72.3.4]

CATHERINE OF LARGS, **William Steven,** from Belfast to Port
Glasgow in May 1682. [NAS.E72.19.5]

CATHERINE OF GREENOCK, **James Scott,** from Dublin to Port
Glasgow in May 1682. [NAS.E72.19.5]

CATHERINE OF IRVINE, **William Scott,** from Belfast to Port
Glasgow in September 1684. [NAS.E72.19.9]

CHARLES OF GLASGOW, **David Smith,** from Ayr to Belfast in
December 1680; from Ayr to Belfast in March 1682; from
Ayr to Belfast on 22 December 1689. [NAS.E72.3.3/6/8]

CHRISTIAN OF KIRKCALDY, **Andrew Rodger,** from Belfast to
Kirkcaldy in August 1672. [NAS.E72.9.10]

DAVID OF AYR, **David Murdoch,** arrived in Ayr on 23 July 1681
from Belfast. [NAS.E72.3.5]

ELIZABETH OF AYR, **William Lone,** from Ayr on 10 November
1666 to Belfast; **John Lamond,** from Ayr on 21 January 1667
to Belfast; from Ayr to Dublin on 12 May 1681; **William
Hunter,** from Belfast to Ayr in March 1684.
[NAS.E72.3.1/6/13]

ELIZABETH OF GREENOCK, **Thomas Rankine,** from Port
Glasgow to Belfast in February 1681, arrived in Port Glasgow
from Craigfergus in July 1681; **John Lyon,** from Port
Glasgow to Belfast in January 1683; **Thomas Duncan,**
arrived in Port Glasgow from Belfast in May 1683; **John
Lyon,** from Drogheda to Port Glasgow in April 1684.
[NAS.E72.19.1/5/8]

ELIZABETH OF GOUROCK, **James McCun,** from Port Glasgow
to Belfast in May 1681, returned in July 1681; **William Lyon,**
from Ireland to Port Glasgow in May 1684.
[NAS.E72.19.1/2/9]

ELIZABETH OF INVERKIP, **Robert Paterson,** from Belfast to
Port Glasgow in April 1684. [NAS.E72.19.9]

ELIZABETH, **Nathaniel Rankin**, from Kirkcudbright to Dublin,
1692. [Dumfries Burgh Records, charter party]

ELLEN OF KINTYRE, **Andrew McLennan,** arrived in Ayr on 27
July 1673 from Ireland. [NAS.E72.3.3]

FORTUNE OF GLASGOW, **John Kerr,** from Port Glasgow to
Belfast in November 1680. [NAS.E72.19.1]

GOOD FORTUNE OF AYR, **John Montgomerie,** from Ayr to Ireland in July 1667. [NAS.E72.3.2]

GOOD INTENTION OF IRVINE, **William Craig,** arrived in Port Glasgow from Ireland in August 1684. [NAS.E72.19.9]

HENRY OF LONDONDERRY, at the port of Irvine in January 21 January 1681. [Irvine Burgh Accounts]

HOPEWELL OF IRVINE, **James Park,** from Belfast to Ayr in December 1672; **James Blair,** from Ireland to Ayr in July 1673. [NAS.E72.3.3]

HOPEWELL OF ARRAN, **William Scott,** from Port Glasgow on 5 May 1681 bound for Belfast. [NAS.E72.19.2]

HOPEWELL OF LARGS, from Ayr on 16 April 1681 bound for Belfast. [NAS.E72.3.6]

HOPEWELL OF ARRAN, **Archibald Scott,** from Craigfergus to Port Glasgow in April 1681; **William Scott,** from Port Glasgow to Belfast in May 1681; **Archibald Scott,** from Carrickfergus to Port Glasgow in June 1681; from Carrickfergus to Port Glasgow in November 1681; from Port Glasgow to Belfast in September 1682; from Belfast to Port Glasgow in November 1682. [NAS.E72.19.1/2/5/6/8]

HOPEWELL OF IRVINE, **John Reid,** from Dublin to Port Glasgow in June 1682. [NAS.E72.19.5]

JAMES OF GLASGOW, **James Scott,** from Port Glasgow to Ireland in November 1680; **Robert McEwan,** from Port Glasgow to Belfast in February 1682. [NAS.E72.19.2/5]

JAMES OF IRVINE, **Robert Stevenson,** from Port Glasgow to Londonderry in November 1680; from Ayr on 20 April 1681 bound for Belfast, arrived in Port Glasgow from Dublin in July 1681. [NAS.E72.3.6; E72.19.1/2]

JAMES OF GREENOCK, **George Campbell,** arrived in Port Glasgow in April 1681 from Dublin; **William Scott,** from Port Glasgow to Londonderry, in September 1682; **George**

Crawford, from Port Glasgow to Belfast in January 1683. [NAS.E72.19.1/6/8]

JANET OF IRVINE, **James Robb,** from Dublin to Port Glasgow in November 1681; **Edward Keir,** from Ayr to Belfast in June 1683. [NAS.E72.19.5; E72.3.12]

JANET OF RENFREW, **Robert Somerville,** from Port Glasgow to Belfast in July 1681, returned in August 1681; from Belfast to Port Glasgow in August 1681, in November 1682, also in October 1683. [NAS.E72.19.2/3/8]

JANET OF GREENOCK, **David Man,** from Belfast to Port Glasgow in November 1682; **John Scott,** from Port Glasgow to Dublin in February 1683. [NAS.E72.19.8/9]

JANET OF AYR, **Alexander Stevenson,** from Ayr to Belfast in June 1684; **John Gibson,** from Belfast to Ayr in January 1686. [NAS.E72.3.13/16]

JANET OF GLASGOW, **James Guthrie,** from Port Glasgow to Dublin in March 1681, returned in May 1681; from Port Glasgow to Dublin in August 1681; from Port Glasgow to Londonderry in May 1682; **Hector Lyal,** from Ireland to Port Glasgow in June 1684. [NAS.E72.19.1/2/4/6/9]

JANET AND MARGARET OF RENFREW, **James Orr,** from Ireland to Port Glasgow in February 1684. [NAS.E72.19.9]

JEAN OF SALTCOATS, **John Cairns,** from Coleraine to Kirkcudbright on 28 July 1673. [NAS.E72.6.2]

JEAN OF IRVINE, **Ninian Crawford,** arrived in Ayr on 29 March 1673 from Lough Larne, Ireland. [NAS.E72.3.3]

JOAN OF DUNBARTON, **William Irving,** from Port Glasgow to Belfast in March 1682; **Arthur Dalgleish,** arrived in Port Glasgow from Belfast in August 1682; **William Irving,** from Port Glasgow to Belfast in November 1682, from Port Patrick to Ireland in March 1683; from Port Glasgow to Belfast in July 1683. [NAS.E72.19.5/8]

JOHN OF SALTCOATS, arrived in Ayr on 28 March 1673 from
Londonderry; **William Martin,** from Port Glasgow to Belfast
in June 1682. [NAS.E72.3.3; E72.19.5]

JOHN OF GREENOCK, **William Hastie,** from Ayr to Dublin in
February 1683, returned in February 1683; **James Rankine,**
from Ayr to Belfast in February 1685. [NAS.E72.3.11/15]

KATHERINE OF GLASGOW, from Glasgow to Belfast in 1690.
[RPCS.XV.88]

MARGARET OF AYR, **John Thomson,** from Ayr on 7 May 1667
to Coleraine; bound from Ayr to Belfast on 25 April 1681;
John Gowan, from Belfast to Ayr in May 1681.
[NAS.E72.3.2/4/6]

MARGARET OF GREENOCK, **John McCun,** from Port Glasgow
to Belfast and Dublin in March 1681, returned in April 1681;
John Lyon, from Port Glasgow to Belfast in April 1681.
[NAS.E72.19.2/8]

MARGARET OF RENFREW, **Adam Cochrane,** from Port
Glasgow to Carrickfergus in May 1681, and to Belfast in July
1681, returned to Port Glasgow from Belfast in July 1683.
[NAS.E72.19.1/2/8]

MARGARET OF GLASGOW, **Archibald McCun,** from Ireland to
Port Glasgow in April 1682; **Archibald McRae,** from Dublin
to Port Glasgow in December 1681, also in June 1682, and in
October 1682; **Donald Johnston,** from Belfast to Port
Glasgow in September 1683. [NAS.E72.19.5/8]

MARGARET OF CUMBRAE, from Ireland to Irvine in 1704.
[MRBI#125]

MARIAN OF GOUROCK, **James Scott,** from Craigfergus to Port
Glasgow in April 1681; from Port Glasgow to Ireland in
March 1683; from Belfast to Port Glasgow in April 1683;
from Belfast to Port Glasgow in April 1684.
[NAS.E72.19.1/8/9]

MARIE OF IRVINE, **Adam Cunningham,** arrived in Ayr from
Coleraine in February 1673; **Adam Ferguson,** arrived in Ayr
from Coleraine in May 1673. [NAS.E72.3.3]

MARIE OF GLASGOW, **Robert Galbraith,** from Port Glasgow to
Ireland in March 1683, returned from Belfast in May 1683.
[NAS.E72.19.3]

MARIE OF GREENOCK, **James McCun,** from Belfast to Ayr in
May 1684. [NAS.E72.3.13]

MARION OF RENFREW, **Adam Ferguson,** from Port Glasgow to
Londonderry in March 1681, returned to Port Glasgow in May
1681, from Port Glasgow to Londonderry in May 1681,
arrived in Port Glasgow in May 1683 from Londonderry,
arrived in Port Glasgow from Londonderry in November
1683, arrived in Port Glasgow in April 1684 from
Londonderry. [NAS.E72.19.5/8/9]

MARY OF AYR, **John Thomson,** from Ayr to Coleraine in May
1667. [NAS.E72.3.2]

MARY OF NEWTON AYR, ... **Carr,** arrived in Ayr during May
1684 from Belfast. [NAS.E72.3.13]

MAYFLOWER OF IRVINE, **James Woodside,** from Ayr to Ireland
in August 1667. [NAS.E72.3.2]

MAYFLOWER OF AYR, arrived in Ayr 21 November 1672 from
Belfast. [NAS.E72.3.3]

MAYFLOWER OF GREENOCK, **James Galbraith,** from Ayr to
Dublin in January 1681, returned to Port Glasgow from
Dublin in April 1681. [NAS.E72.3.6]

MAYFLOWER OF GLASGOW, **Robert Johnstone,** from Port
Glasgow to Dublin in January 1682. [NAS.E72.19.9]

PELICAN OF GLASGOW, **William Craig,** arrived in Port
Glasgow from Dublin in September 1681. [NAS.E72.19.1]

POST OF AYR, **Henry Smith** merchant, from Ayr to Dublin on 18
October 1681. [NAS.E72.3.8]

PROSPERITY OF GLASGOW, **William Adair,** to Londonderry in 1689. [RPCS.XIII.589]

PROVIDENCE OF IRVINE, **William Dean,** from Ayr to Belfast in February 1685. [NAS.E72.19.15]

PROVIDENCE OF SALTCOATS, **Andrew Ramsay,** from Belfast to Ayr in September 1686. [NAS.E72.3.16]

ROBERT OF AYR, **David Murdoch,** from Belfast to Ayr in July 1681. [NAS.E72.3.5]

ROBERT OF GREENOCK, **Robert Crawford,** from Port Glasgow to Belfast in April 1683. [NAS.E72.19.8]

SARAH OF RENFREW, **John Pittilloch,** from Port Glasgow to Londonderry on 10 February 1681. [NAS.E72.19.2]

SWALLOW OF IRVINE, **Robert Cumming,** arrived in Ayr in December 1672 from Belfast. [NAS.E72.3.3]

SWAN OF DUNBARTON, **Arthur Darleith,** from Port Glasgow to Belfast in February 1682. [NAS.E72.19.2]

THREE SWANS OF GLASGOW, **Alexander Hardy,** from Port Glasgow to Lisburn in January 1683. [NAS.E72.19.8]

UNICORN OF GLASGOW, **James Watson,** from Belfast to Glasgow in January 1683. [NAS.E72.19.8]

VENTURE OF AYR, **Edward Keir,** from Ayr to Belfast in June 1683. [NAS.E72.3.16]

WILLIAM OF GREENOCK, **William Simpson,** from Port Glasgow to Carrickfergus on 23 February 1681; from Port Glasgow to Belfast in April 1681, returned in July 1681. [NAS.E72.19.1/2]